NATIONAL INST
SERVICES

T0228321

Volume 21

THE POINT OF ENTRY

THE POINT OF ENTRY

A Study of Client Reception in the
Social Services

ANTHONY S. HALL

Routledge
Taylor & Francis Group

LONDON AND NEW YORK

First published in 1974 by George Allen & Unwin Ltd

This edition first published in 2022
by Routledge
2 Park Square, Milton Park, Abingdon, Oxon OX14 4RN

and by Routledge
605 Third Avenue, New York, NY 10158

Routledge is an imprint of the Taylor & Francis Group, an informa business

British Library Cataloguing in Publication Data
A catalogue record for this book is available from the British Library

ISBN: 978-1-03-203381-5 (Set)
ISBN: 978-1-00-321681-0 (Set) (ebk)
ISBN: 978-1-03-205470-4 (Volume 21) (hbk)
ISBN: 978-1-03-205476-6 (Volume 21) (pbk)
ISBN: 978-1-00-319769-0 (Volume 21) (ebk)

DOI: 10.4324/9781003197690

Publisher's Note
The publisher has gone to great lengths to ensure the quality of this reprint but points out that some imperfections in the original copies may be apparent.

Disclaimer
The publisher has made every effort to trace copyright holders and would welcome correspondence from those they have been unable to trace.

THE POINT OF ENTRY

A STUDY OF
CLIENT RECEPTION IN THE SOCIAL SERVICES

ANTHONY S. HALL

Lecturer in Social Administration, University of Bristol

With a Foreword by
R. A. PARKER
Professor of Social Administration, University of Bristol

London
GEORGE ALLEN & UNWIN LTD
RUSKIN HOUSE   MUSEUM STREET

First published in 1974

© George Allen & Unwin Ltd. 1974

ISBN 0 04 360031 X Hardback
ISBN 0 04 360032 8 Paperback

Printed in Great Britain
in 11 point Fournier type
by Unwin Brothers Limited
The Gresham Press
Old Woking
Surrey

To my parents

FOREWORD

BY PROFESSOR R. A. PARKER

———————

There are some issues in the social services which, it is generally agreed, deserve the closest attention but which somehow fail to get it. No director of social services, for instance, would deny that the reception of people seeking help is important; nor would any of his social workers. Yet reception has rarely been looked at carefully enough to discover what actually happens and why. As a result there has been no way of knowing what the overall effects of reception procedures are or how best they might be improved. Ignorance of what goes on at this sensitive point of contact with people in need is liable to distort any estimation of the nature and extent of that need. What is more, of course, it is frequently when they are first received that people form crucial opinions about the system beyond.

In this book Tony Hall reports on research which examines the reception issues in a new and illuminating fashion. What he has to tell us is of the utmost importance in the provision of the social services; especially so because his evidence is assembled and explored within a conceptual framework. He relates the reception process to the problems of rationing. That is, he asks what part reception plays in reducing the demands upon a service to manageable proportions and how changes in the volume of demand affect that relationship. He also considers how his findings may be understood by reference to the disparities between the assumed role of the receptionist and the practicalities of the day-to-day job in manning the frontier of the organisation. There are some fascinating insights into how the flow of border traffic is handled.

This research was begun before the reorganisation and unification of the personal social services. Although undertaken in former local children's departments its conclusions are entirely relevant to today's situation. This is not only because the problem remains with us but also because hypotheses are put forward about how the process of reception varies in different circumstances. In this sense the study suggests how change for the better might be achieved as well as contributing to the theory of social service organisations.

The book is, moreover, a salutary warning to all of us who are engaged in administering and providing services. The warning is about the dangers of taking things for granted and about the ease with which we slip into an uncritical acceptance of what is to us routine but which to the outsider is new, perplexing and experienced quite differently.

Tony Hall is to be congratulated on writing a perceptive, cogent and *useful* account of the 'point of entry'.

ACKNOWLEDGEMENTS

Many people have played a part in the writing of this book, from its development as an idea in 1968 to the completion of the final draft towards the end of 1973. I would like to thank Adrian Webb and Garth Plowman of the London School of Economics for their valuable assistance and comments at the beginning of the project, and Robin Huws Jones and David Jones of the National Institute for Social Work for their much needed advice and encouragement in the final stages. I am grateful to my wife, Phoebe, who kept me sane when my mental stability as a lone researcher was very much in doubt, and who acted as my sharpest critic. I am particularly indebted to Roy Parker both for his ideas and help at the beginning of the project and for his support and enthusiasm throughout.

Thanks are also due to a large number of long-suffering social workers who answered a lot of questions and spent a great deal of time helping with my research when they had more important things to do. Finally, I must thank the receptionists themselves who have contributed so much to this study. At times my analysis of their activities may seem to imply criticism of their work, and for this I apologise in advance. Most of the reception staff I met during the study were highly committed and caring individuals who were asked to do an impossible job.

Anthony S. Hall
Bristol University
January 1974

CONTENTS

ILLUSTRATIONS

INTRODUCTION: RATIONING, PRIORITIES, AND ACCESS

As most readers of this book will be well aware, social service agencies are constantly faced with requests for their services greatly in excess of the limited resources they have available to meet them. Some form of rationing must take place to determine how these limited resources should be allocated between the many demands being made. This process has been well documented elsewhere.[1] Some rationing methods are obvious and are made explicit by the service providers. Others are less obvious, implicit and frequently not even recognised for what they are. Demands for services may be limited by *eligibility clauses* of various kinds which exclude large groups of potential clients from the ambit of any service: by the imposition of a *charge or fee* for service which potential users cannot afford; by deterring applications through the threat of *stigma*; by the public's *ignorance* of what services are available; by the *complexity* of procedures for application; by the *personal predilection* of service providers themselves; by *deflecting* potential clients to other agencies; and by creating *physical barriers to access* such as failing to locate an area office in an easily accessible place, or by not having a sign outside indicating where it is. Each of these and many other methods are used to reduce the number of demands made for a service to a manageable level. It seems likely that the greater the potential demand, the more such rationing techniques will be in evidence.

As an alternative, or in addition, to restricting access to services in these ways, many departments ration by *dilution*, i.e. by spreading their limited resources very thinly across the board. This usually involves a reduction in the content and/or a lowering in the standards, of the services provided. Dilution minimises the difficult problems of deciding who should receive what services, but it is frequently wasteful as only a few may receive a service which is

---

[1] Parker, R. A., 'Social Administration and Scarcity: The Problem of Rationing', *Social Work* (April 1967), Vol. 24, No. 2, pp. 9–14; Rees, A. M., 'Access to the Personal Health and Welfare Services', *Social and Economic Administration* (January 1972), Vol. 6, No. 1, pp. 34–43; Stevens, A. G., 'Rationing in the Social Services', *The Welfare Officer* (1972).

appropriate to their needs. From my observations of social service department area teams in recent months, dilution appears to be a very common strategy to avoid the traumatic decisions about high and low priority cases.

All of these rationing procedures are ways in which balance is achieved between an excess of demand for services on the one hand, and a limited supply of resources on the other. Many of the techniques act as inefficient and inequitable substitutes for some form of rational decision-making about how resources should be allocated between the range of demands being made. Frequently, as a result, services are received not by those in greatest need (by any definition) but by the most vocal, the most persistent, the most articulate, those better able to understand the workings of bureaucracy, the better educated and so on.

Here we are still discussing demand, and not needs which have yet to be translated into a demand for a service. This is because many social service departments are still able to operate only at the level of 'selecting' service recipients from a demand group and have not yet achieved sufficient slack to enable them to search out needs which are otherwise not being met. Whilst such departments continue to rely on some of the unofficial, inequitable and non-rational methods described, no such slack will ever appear.

Some system of rationing is essential and inevitable because of the shortage of resources and the nature of need. If services are to be effectively directed towards those in greatest need, it is essential to ensure that the problems of achieving balance between supply and demand are faced and not simply left to chance or default. If one is to pay more than lip service to this principle, special attention must be given to the methods by which social service departments ration their services. Whatever rationing methods are chosen, however, they should be tested against three criteria.

First, they should be *rational and systematic*, based on conscious decisions by the service providers about high and low priority needs. In social service departments this responsibility falls squarely upon the fieldworkers in each area team. They are in the best possible position—given the support of their headquarters staff, research departments, directors and committees—to identify and evaluate local needs, to make priority choices and to put them into effect. Whilst committees and directors might be expected to provide the broad outlines of general policy, it would be neither possible nor appropriate for either group to convert these general statements into specific criteria for case acceptance and rejection. This is the professional responsibility of the fieldworkers who make the day-to-day decisions at the point of client intake. Only they have the knowledge and information to make such decisions, and the ability to put them into practice. Second, rationing methods and the criteria used for defining eligibility for services should be *explicit*. Only in this way can decisions about how resources are allocated between various types of need be challenged and changed by staff, consumers, committees and public alike. Finally, it is important that whatever system a department employs for establishing its priorities and making them explicit, there should be regular, and ideally, frequent, opportunities for reviewing, re-examining and evaluating these choices.

However participative the process of defining priorities for service provision, ultimately the task of ensuring that services are provided for those in greatest need rests with the service providers themselves. To attempt to resolve the problem of resource scarcity by informal and non-explicit means, by creating barriers to access and by not taking positive steps to ensure that resources are rationally and effectively distributed, is to abdicate this responsibility.

What follows is a case-study in the process of rationing.

Chapter 1

THE CLIENT
RECEPTION PROCESS

This book describes the client reception process in four children's department offices just before social service reorganisation in 1971. The case studies were undertaken to analyse the effects of reception facilities and the activities of receptionists on the provision of child care services by the social work staff. They show that the reception process is not just an administrative expedient but that, under certain circumstances, it may have a profound influence upon the way an agency operates, the services it provides and who receives them. In short, many of the important rationing decisions about resource allocation may be made not by a department's senior or middle management, or by its professional social work staff, but by a clerical officer at the point of initial contact between the agency and its clients.

These findings are not just relevant to children's departments, but are of even greater importance in the context of modern social service agencies. The general trend towards larger and more powerful organisations, and in particular the 'one door' policy in the personal social services, makes it imperative that the person who opens this door is willing and able to ensure that those asking for help are given an equal opportunity of receiving it.

In writing the book I have been aware of two main audiences. It was originally to be directed at students and teachers of social administration who were particularly concerned with administrative aspects of service provision. As the writing progressed, successive drafts were modified in layout, orientation and language to make it also of interest and, I hope, of value, to fieldworkers, social service administrators and receptionists themselves.

The methodology employed in the study and some of the problems encountered, are described in detail in Chapter 2. Chapters 3 to 6 contain the case-studies of reception practices in four very different settings. Each highlights a particular feature of the reception situation. Chapters 3 and 4 compare and contrast the problems faced by staff when operating under conditions of high and low client bombardment respectively. Chapter 5 is concerned with the different problems and pressures confronting two receptionists working in the same building: one, a general receptionist attending to all callers at a large town hall; the other, a clerk in the children's department area office on the second floor. The last case-study, outlined in Chapter 6, describes the reception process in an office in which the receptionist's role was minimised by explicit and clearly defined office intake procedures.

Finally, Chapter 7 summarises the major features of the client reception and intake processes identified in the case-studies, and considers some of the implications for the reception of visitors to social welfare agencies in general. For the hurried reader, or indolent reviewer, the key points of problem diagnosis and possible remedies are contained within Chapters 3 and 7.

First, by way of introduction, let us consider the rationale for the study and for isolating client reception as being a valid and important area for analysis.

RECEPTION AS THE FIRST POINT OF CONTACT

For any organisation which provides a face-to-face service in an agency setting, the reception of visitors is a basic task. Every such agency must make some form of provision for receiving its clients on arrival and for ensuring that they are seen by a relevant member of the organisation's staff. This task may simply be performed by the service providers themselves, as in the case of the private detective of crime fiction whose clients walk straight into his room. More frequently in formal organisations an intermediary is involved —a third party who is responsible for the three basic elements in the client reception process:

1. Greeting and attending to visitors,
2. Ensuring that the visitor has come to the right place and, if so,
3. Establishing contact (either at the time or in the future) between the service provider and the potential recipient.

In a profit-making service organisation each of these elements in the reception process is of considerable importance. As the clients' initial point of contact with the organisation, the receptionist is the primary source of first impressions. In effect *she* represents the agency in front-line meetings with its public-in-contact. Added to this, the degree of efficiency with which clients are enabled to use the services provided may be largely dependent upon the skill and resources of this intermediary. If any of these tasks is inadequately performed, the profit-making potential of the organisation may be seriously impaired, especially if it is faced with the fierce competition of a rival concern.[1] Consequently, in the private sector considerable resources are invested in ensuring that client reception facilities are as attractive and as administratively efficient as possible.

This concern with the reception of visitors is rarely as well developed in social service agencies. One has only to visit the 'average' social service department waiting-room to get some rough indication of the degree of priority accorded to it. (A simple check for any sceptical reader would be a visit to his or her local office of the Department of Health and Social Security.) And yet there are very good grounds for arguing that client reception is even more important in organisations concerned with social welfare provision.

In a social welfare agency for a variety of historical, social and psychological reasons there is a special kind of relationship between the giver and receiver of services which is not characteristic of profit-orientated service organisations. Mayer Zald distinguishes three features of client-organisation relations in welfare agencies which are not commonly found in other types of organisation.[2] First, 'because the client usually does not buy the service, the agency personnel . . . may be less intent on satisfying the client and meeting his needs'. In other words, the client does not have the advantage of a monetary sanction to ensure a high quality of service from the agency's staff. Second, there is a status differential between clients of the two kinds of organisation. 'Clients in welfare organisations are often not full participants in the society; they frequently come to the agency as supplicants without full rights or means.' Finally, 'client-staff interactions are marked by breakdowns in communications stemming from the differences in

---

[1] For a discussion of such a situation in the dry-cleaning industry see: Miller, E. J. and Rice, A. K., *Systems of Organisation* (Tavistock, 1967), Ch. 7.

[2] Zald, M. N. (ed.), *Social Welfare Institutions; a Sociological Reader* (Wiley, New York, 1965), Introduction to Part D, 'Client Relations', pp. 555–7.

psychological perception and differences in class and educational backgrounds'.

Each of these features helps to produce a client-agency relationship which is characterised by *dependence*. The client is essentially dependent upon the organisation and its staff by virtue of his need for resources which can frequently only be obtained from that source. This relationship has been noted by a number of writers.[1] Joel Handler, for example, argues the point specifically in relation to the child care service:

> 'The children's department stands in a very powerful position *vis-à-vis* the client. The agency is a dispenser of rewards and benefits (which includes the staving off of more serious sanctions) that the families sorely need. These rewards and benefits are levers that the officers use in the casework plan. The casework plan means changing behaviour to conform to what the child care officer thinks is proper. . . . The (ability to apply) coercion stems from the structural position of the agencies (children's departments) which gives them enormous power over clients. Child care officers are authority figures. They are extensions of other authoritative agencies—the police, the schools, the health agencies—or the key to desperately needed benefits. The brokering activities of the children's departments gives them the power to do things that clients want.'[2]

This relationship of dependence is reinforced by the stigma associations which an application to a social welfare agency almost inevitably invokes.[3]

Anticipation of *dependence*, feelings of *stigma*, or simply the state of *uncertainty*[4] as to what will result from an approach to the agency, are only part of the traumatic 'pre-client phase'[5] experienced

---

[1] For example: Forder, A., *Social Casework and Administration* (Faber & Faber, 1966); Rees, A. M., 'Access to the Personal Health and Welfare Services', *Social and Economic Administration* (1972), Vol. 6, No. 1, pp. 34–43.

[2] Handler, J. F., 'The Coercive Children's Officer', *New Society* (3 October 1968), pp. 485–7.

[3] For a discussion of the bases of stigma in social services organisations see: Pinker, R., *Social Theory and Social Policy* (Heinemann, 1971), Ch. 4. (Reproduced in shortened form in 'Stigma and Social Welfare', *Social Work* (October, 1970). Vol. 27, No. 4, pp. 13–17.

[4] Daniel, P., 'Client Stress: Some Implications for Social Work Agencies', *The Voice of the Social Worker* (Family Welfare Association, 1970).

[5] The concept of the 'pre-client phase' is discussed in detail by Landy, D., 'Seeking Help in Our Culture' in Zald, op. cit., pp. 559–74, and Perlman, H. H., *Social Casework: A Problem-Solving Process* (Chicago University Press, 1957).

by many potential applicants for social welfare assistance. Under these circumstances the decision to contact the organisation is often a difficult one.[1] Once the decision is made, the way in which the client is received at the point of initial application and immediately afterwards (the reception and intake process) may be crucial in determining whether or not contact is maintained and the client's needs attended to by the social work staff.

PATTERNS OF CLIENT-AGENCY CONTACT

Chapter 3 is an account of reception practices in a local authority in inner London which, for the sake of anonymity, has been dubbed 'Borough'. This study was initially undertaken as a by-product of a larger survey of new client applications to Borough on which I was engaged between 1968 and 1970. The pattern of new client-agency contacts identified in this study and recorded in detail elsewhere[2] was the reason for my original interest in client reception and intake, and provides a further rationale for closer examination of the work of reception staff.

The survey was undertaken to examine the nature and extent of contacts between a children's department and its new clients. A 'tracer technique' was employed. Social workers in the agency were asked to complete a questionnaire for every new applicant to the department for any form of assistance over a period of six months. Every client in the cohort assembled in this way was traced in their contacts with the department for a further six months. Information was collected for all clients on the length of time they remained in touch with the agency, what services they received, how frequently they made contact, and so on.

The results indicated that a very high proportion of the department's new clients remained in contact for only a short time, that many visited on only one occasion, and that the majority received only 'minimal services'. The basic patterns of contact are shown in Figure 1. A total of 650 new applications were recorded over the six months study period. Of these, 565 (87 per cent) were designated by child care officers as 'closed' only three months after the initial inquiry date; only 85 (13 per cent) remained 'open'. Subse-

---

[1] Mayer, J. E., and Timms, N., *The Client Speaks: Working-Class Impressions of Casework* (Routledge & Kegan Paul, 1970).
[2] Hall, A. S., 'An Analysis of the Work of a Local Authority Children's Department *vis-à-vis* its New Clients' (mimeo., 1970, NISW Library).

quently 40 of the closed cases were re-opened—either as a result of a separate inquiry or a new development connected with the original reason for application. Thus, overall, as many as 525 cases, or 81 per cent of the total number of new clients, were closed within three months of the initial inquiry date and were not re-opened during the study period.

Of the 650 cases in the cohort, only 81 (12 per cent) were still considered to be current case clients six months after the original contact was made with the agency. That is, 88 per cent of all new applications were closed within six months. Clearly, the vast majority of new applications to this particular department were dealt with on a short-term basis only.

At this point it is worth stressing that, if anything, by reason of

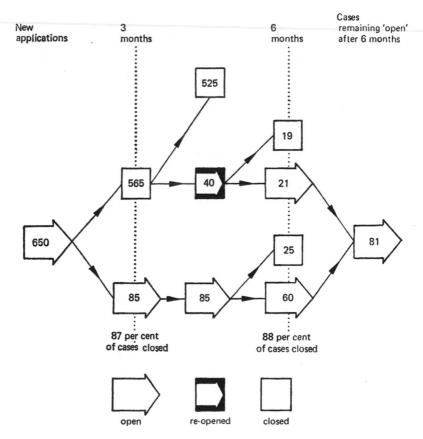

Figure 1   Pattern of Client Flow through Borough

the methods used to ensure an adequate response to the survey, the long-term cases are likely to be over-represented rather than under-represented in the data. For example, if a client was allocated to a social worker, or received a substantive service (such as reception into care, assistance in cash or kind) this was recorded in the department's record system. It was therefore possible to check that for all such cases a questionnaire had been completed at the point of intake and the client included in the cohort. Where no such positive or longer-term response was made, no record was kept and it was therefore more difficult to ensure that such cases had been included in the study group. For this reason alone it seems very possible that the bulk of the non-response to the survey (estimated at between 10–15 per cent) can be accounted for by very short-term applications which child care officers did not consider it 'necessary' or worthwhile to record on a questionnaire, or which they simply forgot. (The majority of these cases did not even appear in the department's duty book.) In addition, an allowance should be made for those new applicants who were not included in the cohort because they were dealt with at the reception desk and were never seen by a social worker.

Data on clients in the cohort was collected only at three points: at the time of initial application, three months after application, and again, six months after the first contact. It is thus impossible to identify just how short the majority of the short-term contacts were. However, some clue to this can be gained from the numbers of client-agency contacts made by clients in the study population during their first three months after applying. The vast majority of the cohort—representing almost 80 per cent of the total survey population—were dealt with in only 'one or two' meetings. Here again the preponderance of short-term cases is very evident.

The same picture emerges when one examines the kinds of services received by these 650 clients. A distinction was made in the survey between 'minimal services' (advice, guidance, assistance or immediate referral elsewhere), and 'substantive services' (financial help, reception into care, intensive casework or similar). In a large majority of cases in the cohort (83 per cent of the total) either 'no action' was taken (15 per cent) or 'only minimal services' were provided (68 per cent). In only 17 per cent of cases was any substantive service provided for clients during their first three months of contact with the agency.

Whatever reasons might be suggested as to why this pattern

of client-agency contact had become established in Borough, it
is quite clear that under these circumstances the department was
operating very largely as an advice centre and broker within the
child care system of which it was a part. In consequence, for a
very large proportion of children's department applicants at that
time, their only experience of the department was of the receptionist
and duty officer. Many did not proceed through the organisation
beyond the reception-intake phase.

This pattern is not peculiar to Borough. A survey conducted
quite independently along similar lines in the late 1960s recorded
similar findings in another urban children's department. Here,
where the numbers were calculated on a slightly different basis,
'40 per cent of all referrals in the city . . . were dealt with on the
day of referral either by giving the clients information or by
linking them with other agencies'.[1] In all, a total of 92 per cent of
applications were concluded on a short-term basis (i.e. were
designated as 'closed' within three months). The similarity of this
figure with the 87 per cent recorded for Borough is striking.

Evidence about client contact patterns in social service departments is sparse, but that which does exist suggests that they deal
with very similar proportions of short-term contacts to those found
in their more specialist predecessors. Two unpublished departmental studies undertaken by course members at the National
Institute for Social Work since reorganisation have both produced
evidence of between 80–90 per cent short-term contacts. A study
of an intake team by T. M. Duncan in the London Borough of
Hammersmith shows that 80 per cent of new referrals were dealt
with on a short-term basis.[2]

The pattern of a high proportion of short-term contacts demonstrated originally in Borough, certainly does not appear to have been
peculiar to Borough, to children's departments, or even to Britain.
The American literature reflects concern about a similar tendency
in social work organisations in the United States, despite considerable differences in the type of agency concerned. A great deal
of attention is directed towards what H. H. Perlman has described
as 'The Case of the Third Man'.[3] This refers to the fact that one-

[1] George, V. and Hazel, N., 'The Work of Two Children's Departments', *Social
Work* (January 1970), Vol. 27, No. 1, pp. 23–5.
[2] Duncan, T. M., 'Intake in an Integrated Team', *Health and Social Services
Journal* (10 February 1973).
[3] Perlman, H. H., 'Intake and Some Role Considerations', *Social Casework*
(USA, April 1960), Vol. 41, No. 4, pp. 171–7.

third of all applicants to social work agencies designated as needing the agencies' casework help do not return after the first interview.[1] It seems reasonable to assume that this proportion would be far greater if those applicants considered *not* to require casework assistance and those merely seeking information or short-term advice were also included in the totals. The problem is seen variously in terms of client misinterpretation of the role of the agency, external pressures on the client to withdraw, and role conflicts between client and worker during the initial intake interview. The focus of attention in each case is the client, the social worker or the relationship between them. However, in most British social work agencies at least, an important part of the intake process is undertaken at the reception desk.

This is not to suggest that inferior reception arrangements and possibly the overt attitudes of a brusque reception worker is the sole or even the major cause of client drop-out, early termination of contacts and the demonstrably high proportion of short-term work undertaken by social work agencies. This would obviously be an absurd proposition. Rather it is to draw attention to the need to examine further the nature of social worker-client contacts and relationships within the agency context.

An obvious starting point is the initial contact between the agency and the client. For clients whose first contact is by telephone the key person may be the telephonist and/or duty officer. For those who make their initial approach to the agency by a personal visit to the office, the first person they meet is likely to be a clerk behind the reception desk. Hence the present study. In the agency setting the receptionist may act as a powerful intermediary between the social worker and the client simply by virtue of her location near to the main entrance.

The potential importance of the receptionist is not restricted to contacts with clients new to the agency. As will be demonstrated continually throughout the chapters which follow, this is extended to those who are already the subjects of current case files. At the

---

[1] The literature on this phenomenon is extensive but essentially incestuous. See for example the following: Shyne, A. W., 'What Research Tells Us about Short-Term Cases in Family Agencies', *Social Casework* (USA, May 1957), Vol. 38, No. 5, pp. 223–31; Ripple, L., 'Motivation, Capacity and Opportunity as Related to the Use of Casework Service', *Social Service Review* (USA, 1955), Vol. 29, No. 2, pp. 172–93; Kogan, L. S., 'The Short-Term Case in a Family Agency', *Social Casework* (in three parts) (USA, May–July 1957), Vol. 38, Nos 5–7; Reid, W. J. and Shyne, A. W., *Brief and Extended Casework* (Columbia University Press, 1969).

simple level of counting heads, in the Borough department as many as 25 per cent of visitors (140 clients in a two-week period for which records were kept) were not seen at all by a social worker. In one of the case-studies undertaken subsequently this proportion was as high as 40 per cent. In these examples the clients' sole contact with the organisation was through the reception staff.

THE RECEPTIONIST AS GATEKEEPER

So far I have been arguing that by virtue of her physical location and role within the service organisation, the receptionist is in a potentially powerful position to influence the nature and extent of transactions between service providers and potential recipients. What evidence exists as to the ways in which this influence can be exercised? To what extent is it used, and with what effect?

Specific references in the literature are sparse and largely unconnected. The few that there are, however, suggest a need for a more systematic analysis of the influence of reception staff in the context of welfare agency operations. The need for further research into the relationship between clerical staff and professional social workers was noted by Burns and Sinclair in 1963. They comment:

'While there is no reason from our evidence to suppose that the involvement of secretarial assistants in the work of the department carried them into the sphere of professional casework, there are many instances in which it might be supposed that people in this position in some smaller authorities were taking a sizeable part in some of the responsibilities usually falling to professional workers. . . . It is no part of our purpose to suggest that rigid demarcation lines should be drawn around the professional workers' sphere of activities, but the role of the secretarial assistant as receptionist and as the professional workers' aide possibly needs re-examination.'[1]

Anthony Forder highlights one way in which a receptionist as gatekeeper might exert an influence on primary service provision. He recounts the often quoted case of a voluntary family casework agency housed in a local government office which discovered the importance of the hall porter in referring clients to them.

'It was the duty of the hall porter to direct callers to the appropriate department. He was well aware that most people who called

[1] Burns, T. and Sinclair, S., *The Child Care Service at Work* (HMSO, 1963).

at the office were very unsure of which was the appropriate department for their needs. To discover where they should go he, in effect, conducted a preliminary interview. While one might say that he was exceeding his duties and doing a job for which he was not properly prepared, it was in fact a necessary job, and there was no one else to do it.'[1]

Similar passing references are made elsewhere.[2]

More recently Robert Bessell went so far as to suggest that:

'Possibly the most important single factor which determines the public image [of a social work agency] is the way in which the agency receives its prospective clients and it is no exaggeration to say that, in many cases, what happens before the client sees the social worker will not only determine the outcome of the interview but whether the client will even be admitted to see a social worker and if he does, whether he will return.'[3]

The evidence presented in this book does much to support Bessell's contention.

One of the few important contributions to an otherwise scant literature, which attempts to identify the true nature of the receptionist's power in an organisation is provided by Irwin Deutscher.[4] In his analysis of the work of the application officer in an American public housing authority, Deutscher extends and develops Kurt Lewin's conception of the gatekeeper's role.[5] Despite certain basic differences in the two situations which will become apparent, the client-orientated activities of the applications officer in the housing authority and reception staff in at least two of the case-studies reported below are very similar.

His basic argument is simple. Man is increasingly required to come into contact with large-scale, bureaucratic organisations. When entering any such organisation a person must encounter

[1] Forder, op. cit., pp. 90–1.
[2] Donnison, D. V., Chapman, V., et al., Social Policy and Administration (Allen & Unwin, 1965), p. 41; Sinfield, A., 'Which Way for Social Work?', Fabian Pamphlet (393), p. 23; Report of the Committee on Local Authority and Allied Personal Social Services (HMSO, 1968), Cmnd 3703, p. 182, para. 585.
[3] Bessell, R., Interviewing and Counselling (Batsford, 1971).
[4] Deutscher, I., 'The Gatekeeper in Public Housing', Among the People: Encounters with the Poor, edited by Deutscher, I., and Thompson, E. J. (Basic Books, New York, 1968).
[5] Lewin, K., 'Frontiers in Group Dynamics: II. Channels of Group Life; Social Planning and Action Research', Human Relations (1947), 1.

some form of gatekeeper 'who will determine just how far he will get and how long it will take him'. This decision

> 'may be a foregone conclusion—a *ritualistic* decision; it may be one that is determined by *tradition*; it may be the whimsical result of a powerful and capricious individual. It is also possible for such decisions to be made according to formal rules and criteria . . . or, for that matter, according to informal rules and criteria. . . . The fact remains that because of his ignorance of such specialised bureaucracies, the common man often finds himself at the mercy of the ubiquitous gatekeeper.'[1]

In the public housing authority the applications officer was the gatekeeper. 'She is the first contact a prospective applicant makes with the bureaucracy. Whether or not the prospective applicant becomes an eligible applicant, whether or not the eligible applicant can hope to become a tenant, and in which project he is most likely to become a tenant . . . all of these depend, in large part, upon the impression he makes on the gatekeeper at the initial contact.'[2]

Deutscher describes the power of the gatekeeper in the housing authority to exercise this level of discretion in decision-making as deriving primarily from two sources. One of these is the official policy of the agency which allows a range of discretionary, subjective assessments to be made by the applications officer as to the applicants' 'need' for housing. Thus 'considerable flexibility is introduced into the gatekeeper's role by subjective official criteria which are often open to a broad range of interpretation'.

Flexibility in the official policy of the agency was further enhanced by a number of unofficial features described by Deutscher as the 'esoteric knowledge' of the gatekeeper. This 'knowledge' has three distinct facets. First, officers in the agency are dependent upon the gatekeeper for selecting 'desirable tenants' for further consideration, i.e. for effectively filtering the total number of applications made on the agency and removing those likely to create difficulties. Second, she is aware of the individual requirements of particular officials for whom she selects clients and clients are selected accordingly. Third, the gatekeeper employs a number of 'tricks of the trade' in order to heighten or lessen the eligibility of applicants for entry to one of the housing projects. 'Through a variety of such informal techniques, the gatekeeper may raise (or lower) an applicant's chances of becoming a tenant.'[3]

[1] Deutscher, op. cit., p. 39.   [2] ibid., p. 40.   [3] ibid., p. 43.

Having identified the sources of the gatekeeper's power, he continues by describing the criteria on which decisions as to whether or not a particular applicant should be promoted for a place in a housing project are based. These were related essentially to the applications officer's own beliefs, prejudices, likes and dislikes. For example, her belief that the development of mixed racial communities would 'create trouble' in the future produced a situation in which all-negro and all-white housing projects were emerging. Thus despite an agency policy of integration, applicants were selected and allocated to specific schemes in part according to the criterion of race.

Again, the gatekeeper strongly disapproved of families without a father present. As a result of this personal moral stance applications from unmarried mothers almost invariably were placed in the rear of the file drawer and 'forgotten'. 'Only once in recent history, according to the gatekeeper has such a person been admitted to a housing project, and this was a special case in which her objections were overruled by higher authority. Otherwise these applicants have no hope of obtaining public housing.'

Finally, each applicant is assessed by the gatekeeper in terms of what Goffman referred to as 'front'[1] and what Deutscher terms 'demeanor'.[2] 'The person's dress, speech, manners, attitudes, and whatever he is able to present about himself during the interview situation are all taken into account by the gatekeeper in her determination of desirability.'

Deutscher's account in this article demonstrates the extent to which a gatekeeper in an organisation is able to exert an influence upon the performance of the agency's primary tasks. It could be argued, however, that this particular gatekeeper is not a typical case. The article is not specific about the extent to which the functions performed by the applications officer are a prescribed and accepted part of her role. But it is clear from the information given that she is more formally involved in the decision-making and client selection process than is the classical clerical receptionist who has very much more circumscribed responsibilities. In this respect Deutscher's gatekeeper has more in common with a service provider than the reception worker acting, in theory at least, merely as an intermediary between provider and recipient. But it is a perfect example of the extent of power which may be

---

[1] Goffman, E., *Presentation of Self in Everyday Life* (Penguin, 1971).
[2] Deutscher, op. cit., p. 46.

C

exercised by someone occupying the position of gatekeeper, and the ways in which this power may be exercised, irrespective of the explicit objectives of the organisation or the intentions of more senior staff.

In the children's department studies, reception staff were considered not as the providers of a service but as aides to the service providers—directing clients to the correct department or room, and informing child care officers and other personnel that a client had arrived to see them. A more direct parallel with this situation is given by Peter Blau in the only other notable attempt to identify the influence of reception workers on agency operations.

Blau directs his attentions specifically towards the work of clerical reception staff in the front office of an employment exchange.[1] These workers were responsible for 'screening' clients. 'They had a list of all occupations for which job openings were currently available. Clients in these occupations (as well as certain other categories who were always served such as handicapped clients) were told by the receptionist to wait for an interview; the others were sent home and given a date for a reappointment.'[2] Rules (the 'due-date' procedure) governed the reappointment date that reception staff had to give to applicants who could not immediately be referred to a job.

Despite the fact that their task was officially well defined in this way, 'all five receptionists interpreted this procedure liberally'. Considerable discretion was exercised. Frequently, earlier appointments were given than were permitted by the rules and occasionally clients were put forward for an interview when they should have been sent home. This phenomenon is interpreted by the observer in terms of the work experience and satisfaction of the receptionists themselves:

'The clerks modified the due-date procedure to make their work experience more satisfactory. Having to refuse clients a badly needed service created conflicts for receptionists who were identified with the service philosophy of the agency and who had experienced the aggression of some clients, who they had sent home. To tell clients, in addition, not to return for two months (the minimum time limit officially designated for certain

[1] Blau, P. M., *The Dynamics of Bureaucracy: A Study of Interpersonal Relations in Two Agencies* (Chicago University Press, revised edn, 1963).
[2] ibid., p. 28.

categories of worker) would have placed the receptionists under severe pressure. By giving earlier due-dates than required, receptionists escaped such conflicts and improved their relationships with applicants . . . . Furthermore, by exercising some discretion when giving due-dates, they transformed a routine, mechanical duty into an interesting social experience. This was partly due to the feeling of power derived from being able to "sneak somebody through (to be interviewed) that really shouldn't get through", and thus help him to get a job, or from determining whether a client might return within a few days or must wait for many weeks.'[1]

Blau interprets this extension of the receptionists' defined role as an example of the principle that officials in actual contact with clients redefine abstract procedures in terms of the exigencies of the situation and the dominant objectives of their task.

'Serving the employment needs of applicants and maintaining good relations with these poor and occasionally excitable people were frequently emphasised objectives of the agency. Orientated in terms of these values, clerks obtained satisfaction from helping clients rather than from exercising their prerogative of rejecting them. This induced them to modify the due-date procedure, in accordance with these objectives, to the extent of defeating its original purpose of limiting the flow of applicants.'[2]

This modification had obvious functional benefits for the reception staff themselves in terms of job satisfaction and diminution of conflict with clients. There were in addition, however, dysfunctional consequences both for clients and the agency. By failing to apply the prescribed criteria for allocating interview dates, more clients came to the agency to be interviewed than could possibly be handled in an equitable way.

Blau makes a further telling point which is of particular relevance and importance in the present context.

'The receptionists' liberal interpretation of the due-date procedure did not interfere with operations directly. Since referrals in this department were based on minimum qualifications, not on selecting the applicants with the highest qualifications, it was

[1] Blau, P. M., *The Dynamics of Bureaucracy: A Study of Interpersonal Relations in Two Agencies*, p. 29.
[2] ibid., p. 30.

operationally irrelevant if one rather than another of the clients meeting the minimal qualifications received a job. As long as the receptionist sent a sufficient number of qualified applicants to be interviewed his exercise of some discretion in the course of screening them did not disturb the placement process. The supervisor made allowances for clerical discretion because it contributed to work satisfaction without disrupting those operations for which he was responsible.'[1]

The employment exchange received many more applications for work than there were jobs available. By the use of discretion the reception staff were able to exercise a considerable influence over which applicants were offered jobs and how long they would have to wait for an interview. To the interviewers responsible for actually allocating applicants to jobs it mattered little, if at all, who the applicants were. The agency continued to operate fully, if inequitably.

The writings of Deutscher and Blau suggest a series of questions about the operation of American social service agencies which could be applied to organisations rather more familiar to the British reader. For example, to what extent does the kind of unofficial rationing and channelling at the point of intake which they describe occur in local authority social service departments? What part do clerical reception staff play in this process? What is the role of the reception worker operating under conditions in which demand for services is constantly in excess of the resources available to meet that demand? Do professional social workers react like Blau's interviewers and fail to question what happens at the point of intake as long as clients are continually coming forward?

UNDERSTANDING ADMINISTRATIVE PROCESSES

The final reason for examining the role of reception is a more personal one. I am increasingly convinced of the importance of achieving a greater understanding of the techniques and processes of administration in the personal social services. Kemeny and Popplestone translate this conviction, and something of the reason why it is held, into question form. 'Why is it', they ask, 'that in spite of the good intentions of the policy of welfare organisations

[1] Blau, P. M., *The Dynamics of Bureaucracy: A Study of Interpersonal Relations in Two Agencies*, pp. 30–1.

a discrepancy tends to emerge between the *official policy* of the welfare organisations and the *practical effect* of its implementation?"[1] (italics added).

Much of the energy expended in the study of social service administration has been concentrated on analyses of the decision-making process, especially as applied to the formulation of particular social policy decisions. Indeed, such studies have provided the basis for social administration as a discipline for many years and are obviously of considerable importance. But of at least equal importance is our understanding of the techniques and administrative problems of translating policy decisions into action. Studies of the development of social policies and, indeed, decision-making theory, may eventually enlighten us as to how and why particular social service policy decisions are made. Only a greater understanding of the administrative process of providing services at the level of client-agency contact can form a basis for effectively putting these policies into practice. In the present context the most that one can hope to do is to demonstrate that however 'liberal' or 'enlightened' is the ideology behind a particular service, this intention can be distorted or totally undermined by the administrative machinery through which the policy is effected.

[1] Kemeny, P. J. and Popplestone, G., 'Client Discrimination in Social Welfare Organisations', *Social Work* (April 1970), Vol. 27, No. 2, pp. 7–15.

Chapter 2

METHODOLOGY

The findings presented in this book are derived from a series of case-studies. This chapter describes how these studies came to be done, what form they took, and some of the practical difficulties encountered during the fieldwork stage. Whilst it is important, and I hope also interesting, to the general reader, it is particularly directed at those who might be involved in studies of a similar kind in the future, whether as researchers or researched.

During the time spent in Borough analysing the patterns of client contact and flow (briefly referred to in Chapter 1[1]), it became increasingly obvious that client reception was a central feature of the agency's operations. This was clearly demonstrated both by early results from the survey, and by observing the methods of work employed by the social work staff. At a time when the survey of new applicants was virtually looking after itself, therefore, I decided to spend several weeks concentrating on the work of the reception office. This was, at the time, only a peripheral interest, not directly related to the main purpose of the study.

Only a few days in the reception room, spent talking to receptionists and visitors, confirmed my suspicions that the reception process was a crucial aspect of the relationship between the agency and its clients. For several months, thereafter, during the latter part of 1969 and early 1970, I made more systematic observations of activities in the reception office, throughout engaging in regular, informal discussions with reception personnel, both individually and in groups.

Having worked in the same rooms as the social work staff for over a year before the reception study even developed as an idea, I had had ample opportunity to observe social workers' reactions to the reception process. Indeed, it was their dealings with

[1] pages 25–30.

receptionists, rationing practices, and discussions between themselves which first alerted me to the possibility of focusing on this aspect of the agency's work. To supplement these extensive observations, I interviewed the majority of child care officers in the department, discussing their work, the intake process, and their relationships with the reception staff. The children's officer, assistant children's officer and senior administrative officer also took part in lengthy interviews. Here the focus of interest was on the development and present organisation of reception facilities.

Two further methods of data collection were employed. The department's records were carefully filtered for any reference to the agency's reception facilities and layout. This provided most of the material on how the reception process had evolved, and on the structure and layout of facilities. In addition, it seemed essential to find some objective measure of the pattern and nature of day-to-day client-agency contact through the reception office to balance against my more subjective observations. For this purpose, over two weeks at the end of the study period, reception staff were asked to complete a short form for every client who entered the reception office. This form (reproduced as Appendix A) required a minimum of basic information to be recorded about each client's visit: name, address, time of arrival, agency required, whether or not the client was seen and by whom, the time at which the client was seen by a social worker or left the building unseen. Much of this data is presented in the following chapters.

Throughout the two-week period during which these forms were completed, I spent most of my time in the reception office. This was partly to ensure a high level of accuracy in the data collected, especially as during the peak hours of heavy bombardment[1] (as reported in the text) such procedures were likely to be by-passed or forgotten as a result of the general pressure of demand. It also proved an admirable opportunity, during slack periods, to discuss the problems of reception in depth with each of the office staff.

[1] The term 'client bombardment' is used throughout to refer to the total number of approaches made to a service agency by its clients, or by third parties on behalf of clients. This includes clients contacting the agency for the first time, those who have had previous contact but who do not constitute a 'current case', and those who are the subjects of current case files. The 'bombardment rate', therefore, is the number of contacts per unit of time. I am reluctant to use the term bombardment in this context because of its military associations, but can find no adequate alternative. *Demand* implies a total service request, and not the numbers of interactions between client and agency involved in meeting that request; the term *contacts* would include interactions in the agency, in clients' homes or elsewhere.

Notes were made during all such discussions and these were written out in full as soon as possible afterwards.

An initial report of the workings of the Borough reception office was produced for the children's department in April 1970, and this was later published in a very much shorter and modified form.[1] An expanded version of this article forms the basis of Chapter 3.

A superficial perusal of the client reception arrangements in a number of other agencies was sufficient to indicate that the Borough situation was far from unique. It was therefore decided to undertake a series of further case-studies of reception activities in a variety of settings. In order to standardise the material collected to some extent, the second-stage organisations selected were also children's department offices. This meant that all the agencies in the study had a very similar range of statutory responsibilities, even if the emphasis and the styles of working varied considerably. The Borough study was of an office in a densely populated urban area. As a contrast the later case-studies were undertaken in more rural surroundings. To minimise the difficulties of researcher-access, the agencies chosen were three area offices of a single county children's department, itself chosen primarily because of its location within reasonable travelling distance of my home and the London School of Economics.

The particular area offices to be studied were selected by the children's officer at my request to include a fairly wide range of circumstances and facilities. Emphasis was placed on variety rather than upon any attempt to select offices which were in some way representative. After consultation, three offices were chosen— here referred to under the pseudonyms of New Town, West County and Cassford—to provide as wide as possible a variation in both size and the circumstances under which they were established.

In terms of size the area offices varied between Cassford with a child care staff of thirty, responsible for a geographical area containing some 185,000 people, to New Town with twelve social workers responsible for a total population of only 64,000. These are the largest and smallest offices in the county. The West County office falls roughly mid-way between these two extremes.

There was also considerable variation in the circumstances under

[1] Hall, A. S., 'Client Reception in a Social Service Agency', *Public Administration* (Spring 1971).

which each office was established and the facilities at their disposal. Cassford was purpose-built as an area children's office in 1962, only eight years before the present study, and had thereafter undergone a number of structural alterations. The West County office was housed in a suite of rooms in a town hall building which, although modern, was not designed for the purpose of child care. New Town child care officers operated from a converted eighteenth-century dwelling house. A comparison of some of the key features of the four case-study offices is included in Appendix B.

The research procedures followed in Borough were repeated in each of the three area offices in the county. Observations, interviews, informal discussions, records analysis and the collection of data on client bombardment in each case took between two and three months.

METHODOLOGICAL PROBLEMS AND ISSUES

The case-studies were undertaken in an attempt to throw light upon a series of very simple and interrelated questions. How does the reception process affect the operations of a social services agency? Does the receptionist influence decisions about who receives what services? If so, what is this influence? How is it exerted, to what extent, and why? It was hoped that despite the small number of cases examined, and the non-random nature of their selection, it would be possible to extract from the comparative data some generalisations about the reception function and its importance in the context of social welfare agencies.

The principal methodology used, despite its inherent difficulties, was non-participant observation.[1] This was chosen not as the best research method available, but rather as the only satisfactory means of collecting the kinds of data required. Where possible, observations and assessments made during the study were tried and tested against more objective sources of data: departmental records, counts of the numbers of clients treated in particular ways and so on. Where this was not feasible within the limitations of the present study, interpretations of sequences of events and practices in the offices were matched against the findings of other, similar studies already published.

[1] For a case-study in the use of this particular methodology see Blau, P. M., *The Dynamics of Bureaucracy: A Study of Interpersonal Relations in Two Agencies* (Chicago University Press, revised edn, 1963).

While every effort was made both during the study and in the presentation of the material to verify the interpretations placed on the observed phenomena, inevitably these interpretations can be no more than hypotheses. It is hoped, however, that they will provide a rather firmer foundation for future work in this field than was available when I started the study in 1968. For the sake of readability, constant reference to the status of many of the interpretations has been omitted from text.

The major and most frequently quoted difficulty faced in non-participant observation studies is the potential influence of the observer's presence on the actions of the subjects being observed—the 'Hawthorne effect'. Inevitably a certain amount of variation and modification of activities will result from the introduction of a research worker into almost any organisational situation. However, although this was perceived as a difficulty, especially in the early stages of each study, it was not considered to be sufficiently influential to invalidate the observations made.

In the case of Borough, as has already been noted, the observation of reception practices was undertaken as a subsidiary project within the main study. I had been working within the department for more than a year before beginning the specific study of reception practices and had come to be regarded very much as part of the furniture. (Indeed by the end of the period in Borough, I had been in the department longer than many of the social work staff.) Most of the observations of client reception practices had been completed before the participants, particularly the child care officers, became aware that such a study was taking place.

The reaction of the agency personnel to my presence in the three area offices in the county presented more problems in this respect. I was admitted to each office specifically to undertake work on a project involving an analysis of the work of the reception office. While considerable effort was made during the introductory meeting and afterwards to minimise the amount of information about the study made available to the staff, some degree of explanation was necessary to gain entry and acceptance. For the most part, however, the study was explained only in very general terms and placed in the broader context of the reorganisation of the social services. This kind of approach appeared to be acceptable.

Blau observes that officials were initially suspicious of his motives because he was introduced by 'top administrators', but that after some time his role as researcher was accepted as genuine by most officials if not all.[1] This was my experience also. Each of the agencies included in the present study had been the subject of a departmental organisation and methods analysis within the previous two years, and some of the anxieties that this had created were regenerated in the early stages. One receptionist in particular, during the first weeks of the study, continually made references in conversation to the 'surprisingly small numbers of visitors today compared with the usual'. Comments such as these continued until she was convinced that my study had not been commissioned to ascertain whether or not she was necessary. (The O and M team had recommended that because of the generally low bombardment on this particular office, she could be deployed on additional filing and typing duties.) When she accepted my credentials she quite openly admitted that 'things were usually pretty slack'.

Despite some early resistance and wariness, both reception staff and child care officers rapidly became accustomed to my presence, and by the end of each study were talking fully and freely about their work problems and experiences. Before starting the case studies in the county offices, some of my experiences in Borough had led me to expect staff to be fairly uninterested, even un-co-operative. I was therefore very pleasantly surprised to find that most people with whom I had any contact were extremely helpful and willing to make a contribution to the study.

A further problem associated with observation studies of any kind, is that of verifying the importance of observed phenomena. Francis and Stone in their study of an employment exchange[2] attempted to underline their observations by measuring the incidence of the practices they observed. Blau in a similar situation applied very much the same kind of technique. At an early stage in the present study it was hoped to be able to use this type of approach to measure the relative incidence of the different reception practices identified. I had intended to assess the extent to which the reception staff used their own initiative in dealing with clients, or conformed to their specified tasks. Unfortunately, the difficulties encountered in attempting to devise such a procedure proved insuperable given the limitations of the available research resources.

[1] Blau, P. M., *The Dynamics of Bureaucracy: A Study of Interpersonal Relations in Two Agencies*, pp. 279–84.

[2] Francis, R. G. and Stone, R. C., *Service and Procedure within a Bureaucracy* (Minneapolis, Minnesota University Press, 1956).

Both Francis and Stone, and Blau were dealing with the numerical incidence of practices which could both be easily observed and counted. In the latter case, for example, the researcher was concerned with assessing the degree of racial discrimination practised at the reception desk in a public office.[1] The numbers of 'coloured' and 'white' clients who were asked to wait for an interview and who were sent home were counted over a period of time. These results were then checked against the colour of the receptionist who made the decisions. In this way some measure of the extent of discrimination was produced. During the study of the first children's department, two possible means of recording the outcome of client-receptionist contacts in this way were considered. I could observe reception practices myself, and record the result of each contact according to the outcome; or, alternatively, the receptionists could be asked to record their own actions in each case. Neither possibility proved to be totally satisfactory.

Recording the results of receptionist activities by the researcher was not feasible because of the complexity of the reception task and the practical problems of observing the reception staff in operation. Each will be considered. First, the activities of the receptionists could not be reduced to the simple, countable actions described in the Blau study in which clients were either asked to wait for an interview or sent home. In attempting to assess the extent of the receptionists' influence on the work of the children's department, it was not sufficient simply to know that a client had or had not been asked to wait. Rather, it was important to discover something of the circumstances surrounding the receptionist's action in each case. For example, was the client asked to wait in response to the child care officer concerned saying he would interview the client, or on the receptionist's insistence despite his initial judgement that he was too busy? In the second case the influence of the receptionists' intervention is rather more significant than in the first. Finer points such as these, which are all-important in a study of this kind, are lost in a straightforward 'head-count', unless suitable differentiation can be made. As the methods of receptionist influence varied over a wide range of more or less 'subtle' techniques, these could not be sufficiently accurately differentiated by a single observer abstracted from the process.

Difficulties of measurement which resulted from the complexity of the reception task were compounded by the practical problems

[1] Blau, op. cit., pp. 87–90.

surrounding any researcher's attempt to record events in sufficient detail to be useful. During periods of heavy bombardment on the Borough office, clients were being seen by all three receptionists concurrently. Some receptionist-client contacts resulted in one or more telephone calls to a child care officer; some required the receptionist herself to provide a service; yet others involved her leaving the reception room to see a third party in connection with the client's visit. Each contact may have been completed in one short interview, or protracted over a morning or a whole day. Recording the outcome of each receptionist interview amidst such a range of activities was not practically possible.

The second method of calculating the incidence of various reception practices—that of asking the reception staff themselves to record their actions—was rejected on the grounds that any change in the responsibilities of the receptionists would be likely to alter the way in which they normally performed their task. This would tend to occur as reception staff modified their actions in accordance with their understanding of the researcher's interests. They would also be unable to record those practices which they themselves did not regard as important, significant or in any way 'out of the ordinary' but which influenced the agency's operations.

The decision not to attempt to collect data in this way was vindicated by one of the findings of the study. A major influence upon the nature of the reception function and the extent of involvement between reception staff and new clients was discovered to be their responsibility for completing a short form on the latter's arrival at the reception desk. Such a form was used in all but one of the agencies to enable the staff to check on any previous reference to a client in the departmental records. To complete this form the receptionists had to conduct an initial interview with the majority of new clients. Significantly, in the one office where the receptionist did not perform this task, the degree of receptionist involvement with clients was minimised. The introduction of a questionnaire, however short, designed to record the receptionists' actions would have produced distortion of their usual practice. Thus whilst my presence undoubtedly had some influence upon the conduct of the reception staff, this was minimal compared with the likely modifications which would have resulted from asking the receptionists to record their own actions.

At the beginning of the project I had intended to ask each child care officer in the four agencies to complete a detailed questionnaire

which would provide systematic information on their attitudes
to the reception process, the agencies' intake policy and facilities.
This too was considered unlikely to produce any useful results.
In all but the first department, the child care staff were well aware
of my research interests and were likely therefore to tailor their
comments accordingly. This was replaced by a series of structured
interviews with a majority of the child care staff in each office,
during which intake, reception, and the organisation of their work
was discussed in some detail. Even in these situations the tendency
towards distortion (perhaps 'selective perception' would be a
kinder description) was obvious in some cases. One area children's
officer, for example, took great trouble to convince me that client
reception had always been a matter of priority in his office. He
explained how his predecessor had chosen the chief clerk to
perform this task, because of her senior position, undoubted
ability and considerable experience. However, in a later discussion
with the clerk concerned, it transpired that this was not exactly
how her responsibility for reception had evolved. She had performed this task for some twenty years having been originally
allocated to it as the junior of the two clerks in a much smaller
office. The question of her not continuing to receive visiting
clients had never arisen. Such accounts were always taken as
indicative of attitudes rather than of fact, unless it was possible to
verify them against other, more reliable, sources such as departmental records.

The methodologies employed throughout the case-studies were
almost entirely geared to what was feasible in the first office
studied—Borough. Ways of recording receptionist activities which
might have been used in one or more of the county offices were
discounted because they would have been impossible in Borough
where the levels of client bombardment were so heavy. It was not
thought to be of any great value to collect data in only one or two
of the offices when comparative information for all four was not
available.

Chapter 3

BOROUGH

This case study describes the work of reception staff operating under conditions of heavy client bombardment. Their observed activities are contrasted with an 'officially approved' or 'manifest'[1] version of the receptionists' role which was generally agreed and recognised within the department. Before looking in detail at the work of the receptionists, however, it is useful to outline briefly the origins and development of reception arrangements in the authority concerned. In this way it is possible to describe the situation as it existed at the time of the study, and to indicate how the client reception process was perceived by senior administrators within Borough.

THE DEVELOPMENT OF RECEPTION FACILITIES

Following reorganisation of local government in Greater London between 1963 and 1965,[2] the health and children's departments of the local authority were divided between a number of separate buildings scattered throughout its area. Early in 1967 the council decided to combine all these sections of the two departments under one roof to occupy the remaining vacant floors of a block of offices in the centre of the borough. The organisation and methods (O and M) unit of the establishment department was called upon to consider the most appropriate way of organising facilities for the reception of visitors to the departments concerned.

On the basis of the team's findings, two important and far-

[1] Administrative concepts may be given four different meanings: 'manifest' (officially approved version), 'assumed' (interpretation offered by individuals concerned), 'extant' (the reality) and 'requisite' (recommended version). Brown, W., *Exploration in Management* (Heinemann, 1960). Quoted and refined by Donnison, D. V. *et al.*, *Social Policy and Administration* (Allen & Unwin, 1965), pp. 32–3.

[2] The London Government Bill received Royal Assent on 31 July 1963. The Act fully came into force on 1 April 1965 after an interim period of adjustment.

reaching decisions were made at this time. The first was to combine the reception requirements of the two departments by having a single reception office staffed by three clerical assistants. This outcome was almost inevitable in view of the specificity of the terms of reference given to the team which called for 'an effective and *integrated* service' (my italics).[1] The second decision concerned the issue of the responsibility for the new office. This problem had not been covered in the O and M report and was therefore subject to negotiation between the leading participants. In discussions with the chief officers concerned, the establishment officer argued that sole responsibility for reception should be that of the department most involved in the use of facilities. On the basis of an analysis of client bombardment rates[2] conducted by O and M, it was agreed that this responsibility should be vested in the health department as the major user.

As a result of these decisions, accepted almost without question by the children's officer and the medical officer of health, no one in the children's department had any direct responsibility for the reception of its clients or for the staff performing this task. The two receptionists who had previously been employed by that department were transferred to the health department. The only issue in dispute throughout the entire proceedings was the grading of the reception supervisor. In the event, the opinion of the establishment officer was accepted by the Finance and Establishment Committee despite the declared opposition of both the children's officer and the medical officer of health.

A number of points should be highlighted from this account. At no time during the course of negotiations were the principles underlying the practice of reception analysed or even discussed. From the outset the arrangement of reception facilities was seen simply as a problem of administrative efficiency coupled with financial considerations and as such was the province of the establishment officer. The staffing of the reception office by clerical personnel was never brought into question, nor indeed was the appropriateness (or otherwise) of the decision to make the health department entirely responsible for their activities. The children's officer made it abundantly clear in discussion that he had never

[1] 'Organisation and Methods Report on Postal, Messenger and Reception Services at —— (Borough)' (September 1967).
[2] See Table 1 and explanation, p. 57.

doubted the validity of these decisions and saw no problems resulting from them.

The nature of the negotiations which determined the reception arrangements at the time of the study serves to demonstrate the role which was attributed to the receptionists. Although the children's officer admitted that they were occasionally involved in dealing with 'difficult' and 'disturbed' clients,[1] their role was seen as essentially 'passive'—important but not exercising any major influence on the agency's work. This assessment was further underlined by the chief officers' declared intention to appoint a uniformed commissionaire to perform part of the reception function. This official would be able, it was argued, to redirect callers to the correct offices and thus 'relieve congestion on the first floor (reception office) during peak periods'.[2]

LOCATION AND LAYOUT

The offices of the children's department were situated near to the junction of two main roads towards the centre of the borough. The department itself occupied the first, fifth and sixth floors of a ten-storey block of offices which rose well above most of the surrounding buildings. The block was shared with the health department, a firm of private architects and a garage.

The entrance to the offices was set well back from the main road at the side of the garage which took up the entire ground floor of the building. The garage concourse, with its petrol-pumps, parked cars and signs, protruded some 15 yards from the front of the block obscuring the small double-doored entrance to the main part of the building. Above the entrance was the name of the office block, but there was no reference to the departments and offices it contained. Indeed the uninitiated could be excused for confusing the entrance to the offices with the garage facilities as the names of both building and garage were the same.

One consequence of this anonymity was a vague understanding amongst residents and agencies in the area, that the building belonged to 'The Council'. As a result potential callers at one or other of the social service agencies in the locality were frequently

---

[1] Minutes of Finance and Establishment Committee, 16 April 1968: Concurrent report by the children's officer.

[2] Draft joint report to children's officer from medical officer of health, 19 September 1968.

D

wrongly directed to the building and were understandably bewildered, and often annoyed, when redirected. During the period spent in the reception office, I noted a number of clients who had initially been incorrectly directed to the welfare department which sheltered under a similar cloak of anonymity nearby. Several of these clients had been so directed by a receptionist at the inquiries desk in the town hall.

The entrance hall immediately inside the main doors was a bleak, forbidding area. Its condition is possibly best illustrated by an extract from a memorandum sent by the firm of private architects to the other tenants of the building:

'The wall surfaces . . . show dirty marks and stains and are impossible to keep clean. Plaster on the walls . . . is chipped at the corners through the movement of furniture in and out of the building and the timber skirting-board is also in bad repair. . . . A solution to the problem of wind and rain blowing into the hall when the rear door is left open must be found. The inquiry office which is unused, must either be removed . . . or locked shut to prevent it from being used as a general refuse store as it is at present.'

Apart from the unused inquiry office, the remainder of the available space was taken up by the foot of the stairs and entrances to the lifts. Just inside the main door was a small sign indicating the floors on which each department was situated, including the information that 'Reception' was on the first floor. If a client failed to see this notice, and it was frequently obscured by waste and building materials after delivery or before removal, he or she had to rely upon being directed to the reception area. The lifts bore no indication of the whereabouts of the reception office, and it was not unusual to find even 'known' clients wandering around the building looking for someone they recognised.

If a client elected to use the stairs, Reception was to be found across the corridor behind two sets of double doors at the top of the second flight. The office was 'labelled' and announced by a variety of different notices and arrows prepared on cards by the reception staff themselves who felt that the single sign provided by the health department was inadequate and ambiguous. Whether the ambiguity remained or whether the profusion of signs itself produced confusion is not clear, but a large number of clients continued to wander into other offices on the same floor asking for directions. The staff of one sector[1] situated near to the reception office claimed to act as a 'Reception for Reception'.

'We get no end of people in here asking where they've got to go. We simply send them back along the corridor. We also get quite a few who object to Reception and call in here in preference. They object to the noise and other clients I suppose. We had one chap call in yesterday who said "Do I *have* to go in there? Can't *you* tell me where the health department is".'

The reception room itself (Figure 2), into which clients were directed, was a poorly furnished area with chairs lining three of its walls, a small table with a few magazines in the centre, and two tables for the use of receptionists at one end carrying telephones several piles of forms. Clients were expected to approach the 'desk' and wait for attention. Under the original scheme the two receptionists were to remain in Reception to be immediately available to receive new arrivals, but the staff had found this to be unworkable. One of them explained why: 'you can't sit out there all day with a sea of faces staring at you, can you?' In preference the receptionists tended to stay in the adjacent post-room in non-peak hours and 'keep an eye on Reception' through the adjoining glass-pannelled door.

At peak hours the office frequently became overcrowded and clients tended to spill out into the corridor whilst queuing for attention or waiting for a child care officer. A few sat down and waited to be asked what they wanted, until they realised that the onus was upon them to ask. (The ambiguities of such a reception situation will have been experienced by most readers in a doctor's waiting-room or in the outpatients' department of a hospital.[2]) When the pressure of bombardment subsided receptionists attempted to ensure that everyone waiting had been attended to.

Few toys were provided for the amusement of the many children who accompanied their parents to the department, and the corridor doubled as an unofficial play area. The head of the O and M team

[1] The social work staff were divided into seven 'Sectors' or area teams each responsible for a distinct geographical area within Borough. All were located centrally in the office block described. Each comprised one small room containing a senior child care officer, and a large room housing the remainder of the child care field staff.

[2] Forsyth, E. and Logan, R., *Gateway or Dividing Line? A Study of Hospital Out-Patients in the 1960s* (Nuffield Provincial Hospitals Trust Series, Oxford University Press, 1968).

which had designed the facilities admitted soon after the scheme was introduced that he had not realised that *children* would be visiting the department.

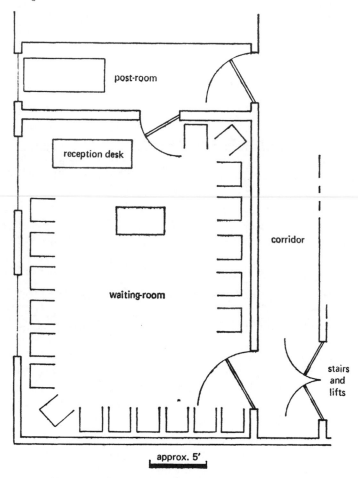

Figure 2   Reception Facilities at Borough (First Floor)

THE DUTIES OF THE RECEPTIONIST

In his study of interpersonal relations in a state employment agency, Blau analyses 'the modification of rules that occur as they are interpreted and applied in a particular situation'.[1] He describes

[1] Blau, P. M., *The Dynamics of Bureaucracy: A Study of Interpersonal Relations in Two Agencies* (Chicago University Press, 1963).

at some length the stringent training programme by which every new recruit to the agency is introduced to the system of formal rules and procedures with which they are expected to comply. Blau continues by means of a functionalist analysis to document the variations from these formal procedures and the effects of this process upon the organisation and the individuals within it.

This was the kind of analysis which I had originally intended to undertake in the Borough reception office. But it soon became apparent that the situation was far less formally structured than that encountered by Blau. No official statement of procedures and principles existed within the department in any easily identifiable form. The original O and M report had contained a brief outline of the proposed duties of reception staff and their supervisor, but at the time of the study only one of the three could remember having seen the document and no copy was available to them. The situation of the reception staff between one department to which they were responsible and from which (in theory) they received their instructions, and a second with which their work was primarily concerned (explained below) produced a vacuum which was rarely, if ever, penetrated by official directive. The supervisor had never seen the O and M report and no attempt had been made to provide her with an account of her duties. Her only instructions as to what the work entailed were introduced in an oblique way during the course of her initial interview for the post some six months before. None of the staff could remember ever having received a written communication relating to any aspect of their work.

In view of the absence of any precise outline of their duties and functions it is perhaps not surprising that none of the staff had received any instruction or training for their work. Principles and procedures were simply passed on by existing staff to any new recruit by word of month. This practice was extended to the new supervisor when she was appointed.

In such an unstructured situation it was difficult to discover any formal procedures governing the reception of clients. The lack of any clearly communicated statement of function from an administrative or supervisory source resulted in the work of receptionists being based almost entirely on an informal code of practice.

What then were the bases of reception activities? As has already been noted, the only 'official' attempt to define the receptionists' role had been seen by only one of the existing staff. However, many of the practices employed were attributed by all the staff to this document. It could be argued that *notions of what the report contained* provided a formal basis of the receptionists' perceived role. The almost total reliance upon word of mouth in interpreting the contents of the report had produced some gross distortions of the original outline, but the staff maintained that they were working essentially within this framework.

A second basis of procedure were the *quasi-formal verbal instructions* given to receptionists by the staff of the departments with which they had contact as to how they should deal with their clients. The child care staff, for example, frequently provided instructions about the treatment of their own clients or those of a particular sector. Interpersonal and intersectoral variations in practice were considerable but over time the reception staff became aware of such variations and attempted to abide by them. Quasi-formal instructions (discussed in greater detail below) formed an important part of the framework of procedures.

The picture would be incomplete without reference to the least tangible but possibly the most important of the bases of procedure. Each of the receptionists made it very clear in discussion that they believed their *own judgement* to be of paramount importance when deciding what to do in particular situations. One summed this up very adequately and concisely when asked about the existence of formal rules: 'No one has ever told us what to do. You just pick it up as you go along. Lets face it . . . reception is just common sense really. . . .'

Given the lack of any readily available statement of formal duties and functions, and the wide range of sources of quasi-formal instructions to receptionists, it was not possible to directly examine the modification of formal rules by informal procedures as did Blau. In a very negative sense, however, there did exist a 'manifest' or 'officially approved' version of the receptionists' role. It was possible in discussions with both senior administrators and social workers to discern a fairly standard explanation of the duties of the receptionist; an explanation which, for the most part, was endorsed by the receptionists themselves. In view of the non-intervention of administrative and other staff one must assume that this widely accepted description of duties and procedures represents the formal framework of practice. It is possible, therefore, to outline this statement of what was believed to be the reception function and to use this as a basis for analysing the observed reality.

The 'manifest functions' of the reception staff can be outlined very simply, and a summary is provided below. The primary task was to receive visitors, to ascertain which department they required (health or children's) and to bring them into contact with the correct official. If a visitor had obviously called at the wrong building the receptionist was expected to redirect them.

A small proportion of visitors to the health department were dealt with by the receptionists themselves. This involved stamping and signing vaccination certificates and similar documents. For the rest—the vast majority of callers—the procedure was to ascertain the nature of the inquiry and to contact the relevant official in one or other department. Clients of the health department, if the officer was available, were to be directed to the correct room on the eighth, ninth or tenth floor of the building.

The procedure for clients of the children's department varied according to whether or not they were already known to the agency. If they were known, the relevant sector was to be contacted by telephone and informed that a client was waiting to see a particular social worker. The client should be asked to wait in the office until collected by the child care officer to go to one of the nearby interviewing rooms. If the child care officer was not at the office or was, for any reason, 'not available' the client should be given the option of waiting, calling back, or of seeing the sector duty officer if the situation was urgent. Clients could be asked to come back later on a specific day, or a choice of days given when the child care officer would be at the office. There was no appointment system as such in operation for clients visiting the department.

Where a client had had no previous contact with the department, the receptionist should record basic information about the client (name, address, number and ages of children) on a 'Record of Inquiry' form. A telephone call should then be made to the records office to see if there was anything known about the client, and only then a call put through to the sector responsible for the area in which the client was resident. 'Unknown' clients were to be seen by the duty officer of that sector.

SUMMARY OF MANIFEST RECEPTION FUNCTIONS

1. Receive visitors
2. Ascertain requirements, and either:
   (i) attend personally to requirements (PH vacc. cards, etc.
       or

(ii) direct visitors to seating area

3. When the children's department is required:

Known clients	Unknown clients
Telephone official.	Complete Record of Inquiry form.
If available ask client to wait until collected.	Telephone records office.
If not available ask client to call back or see duty officer.	Telephone duty officer in relevant sector.
	Ask client to wait until collected.

4. When the health department is required:

Telephone official.
Ascertain if available and
(i) if available direct client to correct room via lift
or
(ii) if not available ask client to call back

MODIFICATIONS OF THE MANIFEST RECEPTION FUNCTION

The observed activities of reception staff differed from the officially approved version of their role for three main reasons. Although classified in this way, these are not altogether mutually exclusive.

1. The *inappropriateness* of the officially approved version
2. The existence of *quasi-formal instructions*
3. The use of *discretion*

The repercussions and unintended consequences of these variations from, and extensions of, the 'official' role expected of receptionists had a profound influence upon the operation of the agency.

1. *The inappropriateness of the officially approved reception function*
The term 'inappropriate' can be applied to the official version of the reception function in two respects. The first of these relates to a general misunderstanding of the conditions faced by the reception staff which had caused the official version to be based, in part at least, on false premises. The second involved the unintended consequences of placing certain duties upon the receptionists—consequences which were considered undesirable by all the

departmental staff interviewed. Each aspect will be discussed in turn.

In the children's department, reception had for the most part operated outside the arena of debate about the activities of the agency. Visitors were received, social workers were told that clients were waiting to see them, and clients were interviewed. As the reception function appeared to be operating smoothly, very little attention had been paid to the work of the reception staff since the office was established at the end of 1967. As a result, I found a very low level of awareness amongst both child care officers and administrative staff of the conditions and bombardment levels faced by the receptionists and of their methods of work. The same lack of understanding could be said to underlie the official version of the reception function. The validity of the assumptions on which this version was based, and the operation of the staff within this framework had never been called into question. The first reason for deviation from the 'official version', therefore, was the general misunderstanding of reception conditions.

One important misconception, which had its roots in the 1967 O and M report, was that a sizeable majority (usually stated to be between 65–75 per cent of the total) of all clients calling at the office wanted the health department; only about one-third to one-quarter were thought to be clients of the children's department. The O and M unit recorded the numbers of clients calling at each of the four sections of the two departments before their amalgamation on the present site. Over a period of one week the average daily total of callers was calculated, and the results are given in Table 1. It was as a result of these figures, and a similar imbalance

Table 1

VOLUME OF BOMBARDMENT ON RECEPTION OFFICES OF BOROUGH CHILDREN'S AND HEALTH DEPARTMENTS OVER ONE WEEK

Department	No. of Visitors	% of Total
Children's	285	40
Health	425	60
Other	not recorded	—
Total	710	100

Source: Organisation and Methods Report on Postal, Messenger and Reception Services. September 1967.

shown in the volumes of incoming and outgoing mail, that the entire responsibility for the new reception office was made that of the health department as the major partner, and the staff were transferred to that department. The continued validity of these results was assumed universally within the children's department, from the chief officer downwards—with the exception of the reception staff themselves.

For two weeks of the present study, the numbers of callers at the reception office were recorded, along with details of the department required. The results show the reverse of the original O and M assessment. As can be seen in Table 2, roughly two-thirds of all visitors to the office wanted the children's department;

Table 2

VOLUME OF BOMBARDMENT ON THE PRESENT BOROUGH
RECEPTION OFFICE—WEEKLY AVERAGE OF TWO WEEKS[a]
1970

Department	No. of Visitors	% of Total
Children's	270	65
Health	124	30
Other	20	5
Total	414	100

[a] Variation between the two weeks' results not significant at 1 % level.
Results of survey conducted by writer.

one-third health. The reason for the discrepancy is fairly straight-forward. Each floor of the office block which was occupied by the health department had its own inquiries office. A majority of clients calling at the building had been there before. Thus 'known' clients tended to go directly to the relevant health inquiries office and by-pass Reception on the first floor. But whatever the reason, the level of client bombardment on the reception office was vastly different from that assumed by the majority of the staff in either department.

The receptionists, on the other hand, were well aware of the preponderance of children's department clients, and as a result were orientated towards the work of that department. They saw themselves primarily as 'working for children's' and had modified the official version of their role accordingly. They performed the duties prescribed by the health department, such as stamping vaccination cards, but other health department clients were dealt with very abruptly. The 'official version' required receptionists to ask all clients to wait in Reception whilst the relevant official was contacted. For health department visitors, however, this procedure was only very rarely followed. They were immediately asked to inquire at one or other of the offices on the eighth and ninth floors, and, it was left to the inquiries clerks in these offices to ascertain whether or not the relevant health official was available.

One result of the receptionists' perception of their role, therefore, was that they underplayed their responsibilities to the health department, and extended their involvement in the work of the children's department. This development was functional for the reception staff in that it helped to clarify their somewhat ambiguous position in the health department and elevated their self-perceived status through the process of specialisation. The potential dysfunctional consequences of this practice for the staff and clients of the health department are obvious.

It is useful to highlight a number of other basic assumptions which were widely held within the department about the bombardment faced by reception staff but which do not appear to coincide with the reality. The first concerns the level of bombardment: the second the proportions of 'known' and 'unknown' clients calling at reception.

Ten child care officers and one assistant children's officer were asked to estimate the total number of callers at Reception over a two-week period. The maximum estimate given was 'around 300'. During the two weeks for which records were kept, claimed by the reception staff to be no different from any other two-week period, a total of 827 calls were made at the office, 539 of which were for the children's department. The discrepancy is probably even larger when one accounts for the way in which the bombardment level was calculated. In all cases where a number of clients calling at the office is quoted, the figures refer to the number of 'client-units' or cases, not to individuals. Thus a single person and a mother, father and six children are both recorded as one client.

It was also widely believed that a majority of children's department clients calling at Reception were previously unknown to the agency. As Table 3 shows, unknown clients represented less than one-fifth of the total number of callers.

The second way in which the 'officially approved version' of the reception function could be deemed to be 'inappropriate' is through the inevitable and unintended consequences of placing certain duties upon the reception staff. This again was in part due to the lack of understanding of the reception situation.

Table 3

'KNOWN' AND 'UNKNOWN' CLIENTS AND CALLS AT BOROUGH
RECEPTION OFFICE OVER TWO WEEKS

	Number of Clients	*% of Total*	*Number of Calls*[a]	*% of Total*
Known	317	80	441	82
Unknown	78	20	98	18
Total	395	100	539	100

[a] Figures include revisits on one or more occasions during each of the two weeks.

The official version of the receptionist's duties required her *to ascertain the requirements of visiting clients.* As has been recorded on a number of occasions, details of the allocation of functions between local authority departments are not widely known among clients and potential clients of the personal social services.[1] Social work staff from a variety of agencies, both central and local, are not generally differentiated but are referred to as 'the man from the Council' or 'the lady from the Welfare'.[2] By the same token, clients approaching the reception office for the first time often did not know which department had the responsibility of dealing with their particular problem. The receptionist's task, therefore, was not simply that of asking the client which department they wanted and putting them in touch with the relevant official. It was one of listening to the client's account of his problem and on this basis deciding which was the responsible agency. For this reason the 'ascertainment function' involved the reception staff in conducting an initial interview. Receptionists took on this task even when a client named the department they wished to contact as they knew from experience that many clients had been wrongly informed, or had made incorrect assumptions, about departmental responsibilities.

[1] See: Timms, N., 'The Public and the Social Worker', *Social Work* (January, 1962), Vol. 19, No. 1, pp. 3–7; Cohen, S., 'Community Understanding of Social Work' (BA dissertation, Witwatersrand University, 1962).
[2] Land, H., *Large Families in London* ('Occasional Papers in Social Administration', Bell, 1970), p. 107.

The 'quasi-official support' given to this practice (discussed in the next section) had led to its gradual development and extension to cover both clients who had had no previous contact with the agency and 'known' clients. In the case of 'unknown' clients in particular, receptionists became involved in deciding not only which department they required but also for which service they ought to apply. For example, when a client informed the receptionist that she wished to have her children received into care this was, on the basis of the information given, the responsibility of the children's department. Occasionally the receptionist did, however, extend her function to ask why, and on the basis of the reply suggest that what was really needed was a day nursery placement. Such a client, if 'persuaded' would then be referred to the health department with his or her 'service request' already formulated. In this type of case—a number of which were observed during the study period—the receptionist was going far beyond the prescribed role, but in a logical development of that role. At the same time the receptionist was providing a service which would rank amongst those normally attributed to the social work staff.

Wilensky and Lebeaux argue that people who apply for social services of various kinds need to conform to what the service providers define as a client. They have to prove their need for the service for which they are applying.

> 'The rules and red tape that swathe the agency within . . . also reach out to mould the client. He has a role to play, too; he must behave like a "case" if he is to use the service. He must fall into certain categories by need or other attribute—a dependent child, over 65, a marital problem, "motivated for treatment".'[1]

By performing this advisory role, the receptionist was assisting the department's clients to request those services for which the department was responsible, and to couch their requests in terms which were most likely to receive a sympathetic response. They were, in effect, helping such clients to 'behave like cases'.

Extension of the 'ascertainment' responsibility was not confined to new clients. It was also applied to some current case clients, especially when the relevant social worker was not available. In the absence of a client's own child care officer it was an accepted practice that he or she should be given the option of calling back later when

[1] Wilensky, H. L. and Lebeaux, C. N., *Industrial Society and Social Welfare* (Collier-Macmillan, 1965), p. 240.

the officer was more likely to be available, or of seeing the duty officer. The option, more often than not, was couched in the terms 'Is it urgent or can it wait?'. The response was usually a detailed account of the problem which the receptionist then assessed as urgent or non-urgent. In this type of case the receipt of the immediate assistance of a social worker was dependent upon the judgement of the reception staff.

The conditions under which reception interviews were conducted were far from ideal. Clients were expected to explain their request to the receptionist on duty in a room which was often crowded with other waiting clients. The opportunities for privacy in such a situation were necessarily limited, especially when the staff failed to see this as a problem. (In one instance of many which could be quoted, a receptionist called across a crowded room to a client, 'When did your wife leave you, Mr ——?'.) This lack of confidentiality could be seen to produce anxiety and distress for a sizeable proportion of the clients interviewed.

The discussion so far has concentrated on those modifications to the formal reception function caused by the inappropriateness of the official version. Such modifications appear to have been the direct consequence of a failure to define accurately the role of reception staff which, in its turn, was the result of incomplete knowledge of reception conditions.

2. The existence of quasi-formal instructions

It has already been suggested that in the absence of any clear definition of responsibility for reception, the staff responded to the quasi-formal instructions of social workers and other personnel with whom they were in immediate contact. These instructions tended to result in extensions of the manifest reception function, and the receptionists themselves accepted their validity, acting upon them in the absence of any contrary directions. At the same time the receptionists were drawn increasingly into the work of the department with which they were primarily involved. Such instructions had a two-fold effect in extending the receptionists' role. In the first place, they had the indirect effect of providing quasi-official approval for procedures and activities which had developed in response to other factors; second, they were directly responsible for the institution of new procedures which extended the formal reception function.

The indirect or 'reinforcing' element can be illustrated with respect to the receptionists' role as initial interviewer. The chief welfare officer, for example, instructed the reception staff to telephone him with a detailed account of the problem of any potential client of his department before referring them on. In asking receptionists to perform this task the officer had not only given his approval to, but was extending, their initial interviewing function. Child care officers provided similar, if less authoritative, incentives for this development by asking the receptionist on duty to supply further details about a particular client before conducting their own interviews.

The unofficial interviewing function of reception staff was further encouraged by the reaction of social workers to the referral of certain clients for interview. There was no official procedure for assessing the performance of receptionists, but the reaction of social workers to their work provided them with an indication of their perceived 'efficiency'. The occasional remark from a child care officer was interpreted as a mild rebuke and had an effect on their subsequent activities. For example, during the study one child care officer informed the duty receptionist that 'Mrs —— who I saw just now didn't want to see me . . . she only wanted a day nursery so I sent her up to health'. The implication in this kind of remark is that the staff of reception were not adequately performing their screening function, and such comments inevitably influenced future practice. In response to these kinds of pressures, reception staff exaggerated their responsibilities even beyond those necessitated by the official and quasi-official instructions on which they operated.

Quasi-formal instructions from child care staff also had a direct influence on the reception function, placing additional tasks upon the receptionist and further defining their framework of operation. It was the general practice of individual child care officers and sectors to instruct reception staff not to disturb them at certain times when clients called at the office. These took the form of 'standing instructions' and 'temporary measures' introduced during particular 'crisis' periods. The object of this practice was to enable child care staff to take an undisturbed lunch-hour or to attend a weekly sector meeting without fear of constant interruption. There was considerable variation in the practices of different sectors. Some would 'close down' for an hour each lunch-time; others made it a general principle to keep at least one officer available at all times to answer 'duty calls'. Several requested no interruptions at all during meetings; other accepted necessary interruptions with varying degrees of 'good grace'.

A major consequence of these individual sector requirements was that the reception staff were made responsible for the regulation of bombardment on different sectors during certain specified periods and, where sector practice dictated, for adjudicating on what constituted 'necessary' interruptions. For the most part they were left with the task of resolving the problem of inaccessibility as and when this situation occurred.

Their response to this additional task of regulating bombardment varied according to the receptionist involved and the attitude of the client. The simplest outlet which was employed in the majority of cases, at least initially, was to explain to the client that the social worker he or she wished to see was not available until a particular time and to give the option of waiting or of calling back later. For some clients who had to 'get back to work in an hour' or had another appointment elsewhere, this option was not sufficient. Difficulties of this type were resolved by the reception staff as the circumstances dictated.

Occasionally they confided in the client, sympathising with the problem and implying criticism of the child care officer for not being available. This kind of reaction was particularly likely when the client had been given an appointment which the officer had failed to keep. Some clients were asked to wait on the pretext that their officer 'will be down in a moment'. On occasions clients themselves were criticised for not keeping a previous appointment and were told to call back. Each response, designed to relieve a possible conflict situation between receptionist and client, clearly shifted the responsibility for the client not being seen on to someone other than the receptionist herself—usually a social worker; occasionally the client. This process is by no means unique. Miller and Rice describe in some detail the very similar reactions of counter clerks in their dry-cleaning agencies. 'Broadly speaking', they conclude, 'the staff of the receiving offices dealt with their ambivalent feelings towards both their customers and their own company by identifying with their customers at the expense of the factory.'[1] Reactions such as these to the daily problems of administering the reception function are discussed more fully in the next section.

[1] Miller, E. J. and Rice, A. K., *Systems of Organisation* (Tavistock, 1967), ch. 7.

3. *The use of discretion*

In analysing this area of variation it is useful to consider the relationship between the reception staff and each of the groups with which they are primarily in contact—clients and social workers. Considerable space in the literature on social work is devoted to the client-worker relationship. In an agency, however, the receptionist acts as an intermediary between these two groups and in certain circumstances exercises a profound influence on the nature of this relationship. There is an inevitable degree of overlap but as far as is possible the importance of the reception function for each group is considered in turn.

The reception function for clients was not limited to that outlined in the official version of the receptionists' role but involved the provision of a range of more positive services. Possibly the most important of these, in terms of the number of clients involved, was the ability and willingness of receptionists to act as advocates on their behalf in contacts with the social work staff. The 'official version' placed the responsibility on receptionists to inform child care officers that clients were waiting to see them. When a client was not seen quickly, however, the receptionist would frequently make further telephone calls, often stressing urgency, in an attempt to speed up the process. Subsequent calls might be made directly, as a simple reminder, or indirectly on the pretext of forgetfulness.

The extent to which a receptionist was prepared to perform this function was dependent on a variety of factors. In large measure it was related to her own assessment of the needs of a particular client, or upon the opinion that he or she was being treated inappropriately or 'unfairly' by a child care officer. It may have depended simply on more personal considerations such as her 'likes' and 'dislikes' of certain individuals. One receptionist, for example, objecting to the length of time a particular client had been kept waiting by a duty officer, remarked: 'I like him. The hours he's sat out there without once getting "stroppy". They [the child care staff] really are terrible. I'll stick up for him. I'll keep ringing them up until they do something.'

While the advocacy function could be an important asset for visiting clients, the reverse process could also be identified. Clients could be 'suppressed' in a variety of ways. As has been described, the receptionist conducted an initial interview identifying the reason for the visit. The subsequent telephone call to the child

E

care officer concerned might be used to exaggerate the urgency of the problem to ensure that the client was seen. Equally, she could understate the problem and cause delay. The outcome was the same when the advocacy function was withdrawn from certain clients to whom the receptionist objected for some reason. Both processes —advocacy and suppression—were clearly illustrated in the response of one receptionist to the question 'Do you treat clients differently for any reason?'.

'No. It doesn't make any difference to me. . . . Well . . . there are those who you feel particularly sorry for, who you think are getting a rough deal. Very often it depends on how hard you push the child care officer or the duty officer as to what gets done. On the other hand, you don't put yourself out for someone who annoys you. Like that woman just now. . . . She'd only been in here five minutes before she asked how long she'd have to wait. I don't like that.'

This phenomenon is not peculiar to Borough. References to an advocacy/suppression function being performed by gatekeepers on behalf of their clients recur in the literature. Deutscher, for example, refers to the applications officer in the housing authority employing 'tricks of the trade' to heighten or lessen an applicant's chance of becoming a tenant.[1] Similarly, Francis and Stone, examining the potential conflict between procedural and service orientations within a bureaucracy, observed the reactions of interviewers in an employment exchange to clients' requests for financial assistance:

'If the interviewers felt that a client deserved compensation they would attempt to aid him, and in such cases considered agency procedures a means to an end of service to the client. If, on the other hand, interviewers felt that clients did not deserve compensation, then they would use the procedures and official rules to sustain their opinions. In many cases decisions were routine and procedure was followed because there was no available alternative.'[2]

[1] Deutscher, I., 'The Gatekeeper in Public Housing', *Among the People: Encounters with the Poor* edited by Deutscher, I., and Thompson, E. J. (Basic Books, New York, 1968), p. 43.
[2] Francis, R. G. and Stone, R. C., *Service and Procedure within a Bureaucracy* (Minneapolis, Minnesota University Press, 1956), p. 127.

In Borough, in the absence of any dominant and well-defined system of rules, the service orientation of the receptionists far outweighed any bureaucratic tendency to become dedicated exclusively to the agency's procedural system. As a result the potential conflict between procedural and service orientation did not arise. However, the reception staff did occasionally fall back upon the stereotype of the 'procedure-bound bureaucracy' as a means of justifying their own inaction or the withdrawal of reception services. This was used partly as a self-protection device and was characterised by comments such as, 'I'd like to help but I really can't disturb the meeting' or 'I would, but we're not allowed to'.

A second important 'reception service' was the provision of advice and guidance. Reception staff were constantly faced with the problem of dealing with clients when no child care officer was available to see them. The lack of any specific appointments system coupled with other factors such as the high mobility of officers in the course of their work, resulted in a large number of wasted visits by clients to the office. During the two-week period for which records were collected, one in four calls at the reception office by clients of the children's department did not result in an interview with a child care officer. In addition, over one-third of all those current case clients who were seen by a member of the social work staff saw the duty officer rather than their own child care officer. I have already mentioned the range of negative responses employed by reception staff in this situation to deflect the expression of client-dissatisfaction with the agency from themselves on to the social worker or even the client. Far more frequently the reaction was a positive one: an attempt to provide a service for the client in the absence of the help of a social worker. This may simply have involved the receptionist trying to ensure that the officer saw the client at the earliest possible opportunity. It may have involved advising the client of other agencies which might be able to offer assistance, or even providing advice and guidance on the problem facing the client. This advisory role is a further logical extension of the initial interviewing function. Where a client had explained 'her' problems to the receptionist and a child care officer was unable to see her, the natural reaction of the receptionist was to advise as best she could in the absence of more professional assistance.

The work of the receptionists brought them constantly into

contact with social workers in the agency. For most of the time the relationship between these two groups was cordial. Each recognised that the other had a valuable part to play, although, by and large, they misunderstood how important their respective roles were, or what they entailed in practice. This caused some difficulties.

The primary task of the reception staff was to ensure contact between officer and client. Achievement of this goal might be possible with a single telephone call to the officer; it might involve persistent calls before the client was eventually seen. The social worker saw interviews with clients who called at the office as only a small part of their day-to-day work. In a situation where an officer was already deeply involved with several cases, and a constant 'barrage' of paper work, interviewing a client in Reception was considered more of an 'inconvenience' than a primary duty. This reaction was particularly acute amongst sector duty officers who were concerned not only with their own cases but with new ones as they arose. Under these circumstances a visiting client might receive rather less attention than the reception staff thought they deserved.

For the receptionist, the visiting client was her sole responsibility and, therefore, the major priority; for the social worker in the sector, priorities were somewhat different. The potential for conflict and abuse of procedures in such a situation was considerable, not least because of the lack of understanding by both parties of the problems faced by the other.

The social worker, faced with other problems on a duty day, tended to place the greater part of the responsibility for clients visiting the department upon the reception staff. This was perceived by the latter group as an attempt by the child care officer to abdicate 'his' responsibility for visitors. All the receptionists admitted considerable problems in this connection in their relationships with the social work staff. As one of the receptionists explained: 'Most of them are very good, but some do tend to take liberties.' It is interesting to note the nature of some of 'the liberties' taken by child care officers. A few were criticised for being 'very offhand', with visiting clients, especially those previously unknown to the agency. Frequently the receptionist was told to refer the client on to another agency. 'It depends on the child care officer on duty. Some ask to see anyone with children. Some tell us to refer clients on without even seeing them.'

A variety of criticisms were levelled at social workers concerning the recording of their future movements. Serious problems were created for the reception staff when officers failed to complete the sector diary. They continually had to explain to clients that their child care officer was not available and that they did not know when he or she would be. The problems were increased when an officer provided a client with an appointment which the officer then failed to keep. Inaccurate recording of their movements by child care officers not infrequently resulted in receptionists asking clients to call back only to find that the officer they required to see was, again, not available.

Other remarks were made about occasions when social workers got them to do their 'dirty work' for them. It was not uncommon for an officer to ring the receptionist to say that he or she did not want to see a particular client that day. The receptionist was given the task of telling the client that their officer was not in or unavailable. 'One case I remember was when a child care officer asked me over the phone to tell a client that she wasn't going to receive her children into care. It's a bit much, isn't it.'

Each of these criticisms directed at the field staff can be seen to fulfil two criteria. First, in the opinion of the receptionist, the client was being treated unfairly or inappropriately; second, the officers' action (or inaction) placed the responsibility for dealing with some clients upon the reception staff. The receptionist might be able to exercise some influence over the child care officer by acting on a client's behalf but only within the limits of manipulating a relationship in which she is subordinate. These limits were revealed in cases where the child care officer decided to place the onus of responsibility upon the receptionist. This might involve the provision of a service which the reception staff considered to be the duty of a child care officer; frequently it placed them in a potential conflict situation which they then had to resolve. For at least some social workers the existence of Reception permitted the delegation of certain responsibilities which they themselves, for a variety of reasons, were unable or unwilling to fulfil. Perhaps paradoxically this practice also had functional aspects for reception staff, despite their declared criticisms. This informal extension of their discretionary powers helped to increase their own job satisfaction whilst at the same time making it easier to deal with difficult situations when they arose. In the process the reception function took on further facets which were seldom officially recognised.

DISCUSSION

Receptionists in Borough were subject to a number of pressures to extend their functions in the ways described. As a result, they became far more involved with visiting clients than was generally recognised or, when recognised, was considered desirable within the department. The basic element in this involvement was the development of the receptionists' initial interviewing activities. These, it was argued, were in part an inevitable unintended consequence of placing certain duties on the staff at the point of reception. For example, the tasks of 'ascertaining the requirements of visitors', and of providing information to social workers about visitors, all created a situation in which the receptionists found it impossible not to be drawn into a discussion about the details of clients' problems. Once they had established such a relationship, however temporary or transient, further involvement, including the provision of 'reception services', followed. (Throughout the rest of this book the term 'receptionist-client involvement', or just 'involvement' will be used to cover all those elements of the reception function which involve interaction between receptionist and visitors over and above the minimum necessary to establish contact between a service provider and a potential recipient.)

In addition to procedural pressures, the tendency for receptionist-client involvement was greatly increased by the high level of client bombardment with which the office was faced. As was described in general terms in Chapter I and exemplified in the Borough study, a key element in the reception process is the task of establishing contact, either at the time or in the future, between the service provider and potential recipients. Many of the pressures for extension and modification of their function were as a direct result of the difficulties experienced by reception staff in accomplishing this task. The conditions of heavy bombardment under which they were operating in Borough served to intensify the inherent problems in ensuring such contact. One could hypothesise that the greater the difficulty experienced by reception staff in linking provider and potential recipients, the greater will be the modification and extension of the basic reception function.

Receptionists in Borough constantly tackled the difficulties of establishing client-worker contact. It is worthwhile at this stage reiterating and clarifying some of the main reasons for this in the context of a high bombardment agency. These are not exhaustive or mutually exclusive but they give some indication of the number and type of variables which need to be taken into account when considering the phenomenon of receptionist-client involvement.

First, for a variety of reasons, some of which have been touched on in the text, social workers in Borough gave a fairly low priority to seeing visitors at the office. This was partly as a result of their orientation towards clients already on their caseload, and the lack of any official mechanisms and policy for rationing a very high level of demand. In consequence, the social work staff themselves applied a range of informal rationing mechanisms which threw the onus of responsibility for visitors back on to the reception office. These included such techniques as asking a colleague to tell the receptionist that they were out or with another client, leaving the telephone from Reception to ring unanswered, and asking the receptionists to tell a client to 'call back later' at some unspecified time. On hearing that one of her clients was in Reception, one child care officer, on occasions, would don her hat and coat and explain to the client that she was unable to talk as she had been called out unexpectedly. Once the client had withdrawn, the social worker returned to the sector office and took up her work or lunch where she had left it.

Another informal rationing device, which in part explains the high rate of office visiting by clients, was the standard response to a telephone inquiry. Inquirers were usually asked not to discuss anything over the telephone, but to call at the office when they were next in the vicinity. After one such response the officer concerned explained:

'We always ask them to call in if they haven't been in [to the office] before. Half of them never do. If they're *really* in trouble they'll make the effort to find us. Either way, if they do come, there's a pretty good chance that someone else will be on duty and have to deal [with the problem]. . . . That's pretty blunt, but it's how most people react.'

Here one social worker was making explicit a practice in which most of his colleagues indulged, although few would have admitted to his particular interpretation. The same worker justified his reaction to new clients by saying that he was unable to take on any more work. If he interviewed a client, he argued, this created the expectation that help would be forthcoming. To avoid this he had to ensure that his contact with new clients was kept to a minimum. 'I'd rather Mrs —— in Reception explained to them nicely that there was no one around, than have to disappoint caller after caller by admitting that we were not able to help.' This was an extreme reaction, and again it is rare that the social worker concerned was willing to make it so explicit. But all the child care staff had developed their own techniques for dealing with the problem of heavy bombardment.

Second, social workers were constantly criticised by reception staff and others for failing to record their future whereabouts in the sector diaries. These were intended to provide all concerned with accurate information as to when a particular child care officer could be contacted. Receptionists relied heavily on this information when asking clients to call back. Partly intentionally as another rationing device, and partly as a result of the unpredictability of child care work, the diary records were seldom up to date or accurate. This exacerbated the receptionists' problems of ensuring contact at a date in the future.

Establishing contact was further frustrated by the large numbers of social workers involved and the physical layout of the building in which they worked. Both made it impossible to keep track of the comings and goings of the social work staff as might be possible for a small area team. The reception office was not located by a main entrance and therefore there was no means of observing child care officers entering and leaving the building. Nor was it common practice (although a few did so) to inform Reception before going out. This problem was increased by the dispersal of staff within the large office block. To consult colleagues, to collect a record, or to visit a senior member of the department all necessitated a social worker leaving his office and being difficult to trace. The number of clients in Reception at any one time made it impossible for reception staff to spend a long time with every client if their social worker was not readily available. In this situation choices were made as to which clients should be helped, whether through advocacy or the provision of a reception service.

For these and other reasons explained in the text, receptionists found great difficulty in establishing contact with a social worker in a large number of cases. In the two-week recording period, one quarter of all visitors did not see a social worker. In many more contact was achieved only with difficulty.

Throughout this discussion the high level of bombardment on

the reception office has been shown to increase the difficulties faced. This was exacerbated in Borough by the failure of staff to recognise the exact nature and extent of this bombardment and to reflect it in the numbers of duty officers available at any one time. It was suggested at the time of the study that despite a large number of visiting clients, there were more than enough social workers in the department—around 50—to cope with the numbers. Proportionately, therefore, a bombardment of 300 clients on such an office is no greater than 36 on an area office with 6 social workers. In such an argument, one point is usually forgotten or glossed over. Whether an agency employs 50 social workers or only 6, all visitors calling to see a social worker are channelled through a single reception office. With only a few visitors to a small agency, contact with a social worker is achieved by the receptionist with comparative ease. There is time to spend on each inquiry ensuring that the visitor's query is understood, finding the necessary papers or file and tracing the whereabouts of the relevant social worker. When the number of visitors is as large as it was in Borough, and given the practices of social work staff in rationing the demands made upon them, reception personnel are faced with a very difficult task. Even with two, and sometimes three, receptionists on duty at any one time, the sheer weight of numbers necessitated reception staff taking independent action and extending the basic reception function in a considerable proportion of cases.

In analysing the reception function in Borough it has been useful to distinguish between the formally prescribed duties of reception staff and the observed reality—what they actually did. In the absence of any written statement of their responsibilities it was necessary to compare their actions with a 'general view' held by staff in the department as to what the job of reception entailed. While useful as an analytical device to highlight the extent of the lack of understanding of the receptionists' role within the agency and to provide a basis for analysis, this technique is not employed in the three studies which follow.

I was reluctant to retain the theoretical distinction, once proposed, between the formal and the informal aspects of an organisation. This dichotomy has now largely been discredited by contemporary organisation theorists.[1] The inadequacy of this distinction

[1] Gouldner, A. W., 'Organisational Analysis', R. K. Merton (ed.), *Sociology Today* (Basic Books, New York, 1959) *and* Etzioni, A., 'Two Approaches to Organisational Analysis: A Critique and A Suggestion', *Administrative Science Quarterly* (1960), Vol. 5, pp. 257–78.

was borne out by the practical difficulties involved in trying to apply it. It proved to be impossible even to begin to distinguish between the two in any of the other offices studied. This can be explained in terms of the notion of social distance. In Borough the social distance between senior administrators and receptionists was great, with very little intercommunication either personally or in the course of daily work. Within each of the county offices contact between receptionists and the area officer responsible for determining the receptionists' responsibilities was continuous and frequent. In short, there was far less opportunity for the area officers to get out of touch with the reception process, and therefore their descriptions of the reception function more closely reflected the observed reality than any long forgotten job description.

For these reasons, in the chapters which follow reception practices in New Town, West County and Cassford are compared and contrasted with those already described for Borough.

Chapter 4

NEW TOWN

In 1948 New Town, a small settlement of some 7,000 people, was part of the North County District for education and child care purposes. With its growth as a post-war new town, the geographical division of responsibility between the various area officers of the children's department had to be brought under review and revised. A separate office was established: first to cover the area of the New Town Urban District Council, and later to include the town itself and outlying villages which regard New Town as their local commercial and social centre. Together these settlements account for a total population of about 64,000.

When the New Town children's office was first established as a separate entity in the early 1960s, it was sited in the premises of the education department. The space was available and at that time the number of social work staff to be accommodated was small. During the 1960s, however, a steady increase in the number of child care officers, together with changes in the department's work following the Children and Young Persons Act, 1963, made it necessary to consider a different location which would allow for the new circumstances and for future expansion. A site was selected—a vacant eighteenth-century building adjacent to the local education office—and the move was undertaken in January 1968.

In terms of client access the new office was far from ideal. The building was sited in the oldest part of the town on the perimeter of the New Town catchment area. Considerable travelling distance, coupled with an irregular bus service, made a journey to the office a difficult and time-consuming process for many clients and potential clients of the department. Despite an awareness of the disadvantages of such a location, it was argued that the shortage of suitable facilities at reasonable cost elsewhere in the area made a more central site impossible. As a result, much of the work of the agency was undertaken either over the telephone or by domiciliary visits, rather than by encouraging clients to call at the office.[1] This method of conducting the agency's work, so very different from that employed in Borough, is reflected in the size and pattern of client bombardment on the office (see Table 4).

At the time of the study the area children's office was staffed by an area children's officer, two senior social workers, ten child care officers and trainees and a clerical staff of six.

THE DEVELOPMENT OF RECEPTION FACILITIES

During the period in which the children's department staff were housed in the offices of the education division—immediately prior to their move to the present site—no special intake facilities were provided for the reception of visiting clients. Visitors to the building entered the general office and were attended to by any member of the clerical staff who happened to be 'free' at the time. No 'duty system' as such was in operation: urgent calls and new cases were dealt with when they arose by any child care officer who was available. The area officer explained that 'in the early days' the numbers of visitors and duty calls did not warrant the establishment of separate facilities, and that even if they had, the physical shortage of space would not have permitted it.

With expansion the area team moved to the present building. The area officer, conscious of past inadequacies in reception facilities and procedures, was determined to ensure that the same shortcomings did not recur. A duty system was established so that there was always a member of the child care staff available to deal with inquiries during office hours—the duty officer. Each child care officer was expected, on the basis of a rota system, to be on duty for a minimum of half a day in each week.

In addition, for the first time, attention could be given to the problem of client reception. The arrangement of rooms on the ground floor was considered by the area children's officer to be ideal for use as reception- and waiting-rooms. Little conversion was necessary. A receptionist could be located in a small room near to the main entrance, and an adjacent area formed an ideal waiting-room. The relatively small number of visitors enabled the roles of

[1] A similar pattern of client-worker contact was indicated for a selection of local authorities in Grey, E., *Workloads in Children's Departments* (HMSO, 1969). The majority of time spent in discussion with clients was during home visits 63 per cent, a further 19 per cent was spent in the agency, 7 per cent in residential homes or schools and 10 per cent elsewhere.

receptionist and telephonist to be combined, so that one person was able to take responsibility both for the telephone switchboard and for the reception 'window'. This arrangement is shown in Figure 3. The area officer admitted that there had been a large

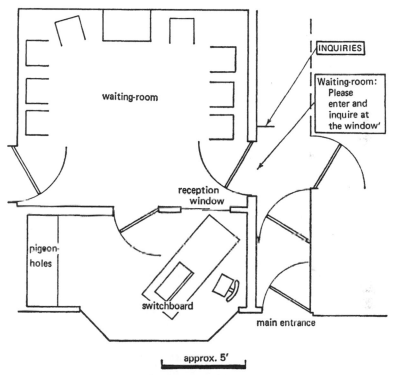

Figure 3   Reception Facilities at New Town

element of chance in providing a receptionist at all: 'We've never had enough callers to warrant a separate receptionist . . . we were lucky that we needed our own telephonist . . . [and that] we could place her near to the front door.'

Less than one year after the move, the county's Management Services Unit (MSU) was asked to review the clerical and secretarial establishment of area children's offices. This was undertaken during 1968 with a view to devising a new clerical staffing formula on which to base future increases in the complement of clerical staff in each office. The reception of visitors and telephone calls was part of the whole range of functions which were brought under consideration.

For several weeks the MSU team collected records and observed the work of clerical staff in three of the county's eight area offices. By asking the staff to record their own activities during the course of a week, they calculated the length of time spent on each of the various tasks performed. In one office, telephonist and receptionist duties were calculated as taking up 1·15 hours and 1·63 hours respectively in a week out of a total of between 220–30 'clerical hours' worked. On this basis it was suggested by the MSU that the telephonist-receptionist in the New Town office was under-employed and a complete reorganisation of the reception arrangements was recommended.

> 'The existing office layout at [New Town] places the *switchboard operator* in a position where she is unable to undertake any other clerical tasks apart from the occasional copy-typing. We suggest that the adjoining waiting room is converted to a file room. This will allow the switchboard operator to undertake file work. The existing file room could then be used by the finance clerk and the vacated finance office used as a waiting room.' (My italics)[1]

Such a modification of the reception arrangements would have had a number of ramifications which were immediately evident to the social work staff. A primary concern was that visitors would be expected to congregate in the agency's filing-room, whilst waiting to be seen by the receptionist. Quite apart from their concern about the unwelcoming appearance of such a room, the staff were worried about maintaining the confidentiality of clients' files. Unless elaborate precautions were instituted, involving the continuous use of keys to lock and unlock filing cabinets throughout the working day, any visitor could easily 'browse' amongst confidential material.

In addition, the MSU had demonstrated little understanding of the receptionist-telephonist role in a client-orientated agency. Although only a relatively short time was spent in actual contact with clients, this role necessitated her being generally and readily available should the telephone ring or a client arrive. The time spent in answering the telephone or attending to visitors could not, as the report seemed to imply, be concentrated into the first three hours on a Monday morning, thus leaving the rest of the

[1] —— County Council, 'A survey of Area Children's Offices' (Management Services Unit, December 1968).

week free for other work. If other activities such as filing had been added to the receptionist's responsibilities this would have meant that for long periods the switchboard and reception window were left unattended. Typing, the compilation of statistics and telephone-based secretarial duties, such as the securing of 'numbers' for social workers and making simple inquiries, were some of the few tasks she could undertake whilst remaining always on hand when required.

For these reasons the MSU recommendations met with an immediate storm of protest from the area children's officer and her staff. Objections were raised 'in the strongest possible terms'. The protest was accepted by the establishment officer and the children's officer, the recommendation did not appear in the final draft of the MSU report and the status quo in New Town was maintained.

Two important points emerge. One relates to the attitude of personnel within the office to client reception; the second to the application of work study efficiency criteria to the evaluation of procedures within a social welfare agency. First, the child care staff in New Town demonstrated a far greater awareness of the importance of client reception than was evident in Borough. Considerable thought had been given to the practical problems of planning the layout of facilities and the deployment of personnel even before the move to the present office was undertaken. Once established, strenuous opposition was forthcoming when the MSU team recommendations were expected to produce 'a far less satisfactory arrangement'. In Borough, the layout of reception facilities and the use of the available staff was devised by the council's O and M unit and agreed by the chief officers concerned, primarily on the basis of administrative efficiency and cost. At no stage in the process were the professional staff of the agency involved in the decision-making process. Responsibility for day-to-day office management in New Town, on the other hand, was delegated to each area children's officer: decisions on the layout and the role of reception were made by the child care staff themselves, on the basis of what was considered desirable from the point of view of providing a 'good' service to clients. The attempt by the MSU to apply other, and less relevant, criteria to the practice of client reception was rejected.

This leads to the second and more general point. The straightforward application of the work study criterion of efficiency to the operations of a social service organisation may take little account of the special nature of the tasks being performed. The main principles of work measurement were developed by the 'scientific management' school initially for use in the context of industrial organisations. As Gilbert Smith has pointed out: 'Although we can learn a good deal about social work organisations through propositions about the general similarities between organisations, there are clearly important differences between types of organisation. To ignore this is to invite error.'[1] All too frequently analyses of organisational phenomena are conducted as if there was a universal model of an organisation which can be applied to any organisation whatever its type or purpose. The most commonly used is the model of the industrial enterprise where it is assumed, in the classical tradition, that the organisation exists to maximise productive efficiency in the interests of increased output and therefore profit. But, in Etzioni's words: 'Policy recommendations based on such a "universal" model can lead to ill-advised action. Consultants working with one of the universal models . . . tend to recommend changes designed to bring the organisation into line with the model.'[2] Two examples of this danger on a small scale have been described. In Borough the O and M unit were not fully aware of the role to be performed by the reception staff or of the problems they would be facing. As a result a range of dysfunctional unintended consequences were faced by both clients and social workers in the departments concerned. In New Town the MSU's perception of the receptionist simply as a switchboard operator denied the special client-orientated nature of this particular task. In both cases the application of non-service criteria to the measurement and evaluation of the performance of reception staff produced a situation in which the reception function was undervalued and potentially undermined.

THE CONTEXT OF CLIENT RECEPTION IN NEW TOWN

To present a straightforward description of the work of the receptionist in the New Town office immediately following an analysis of reception practices in Borough, would be misleading without first highlighting certain basic differences in the circumstances in which the reception function was being performed in

[1] Smith, G., *Social Work and the Sociology of Organisations*, 'Library of Social Work' (Routledge & Kegan Paul, 1970), p. 13.
[2] Etzioni, A., *A Comparative Analysis of Complex Organisations* (Free Press, New York, 1961, p. xiii; Collier-Macmillan, 1972).

the two offices. Given that in both cases reception facilities were manned by clerical personnel and that both agencies were offices of a children's department, the two cases could hardly be more dissimilar. A comparison between these two very different situations provides not only a background against which to view the reception practices in the New Town office, but also a number of hypotheses about how and why variations occur in the activities of reception staff. These are presented in the discussion at the end of this chapter. But first let us examine three differences between Borough and New Town which significantly influence the nature of their reception processes. These are differences between the agencies themselves, variations in the levels of client bombardment and in the reception facilities provided.

DIFFERENCES BETWEEN THE AGENCIES

The Borough children's department was a single agency responsible for the provision of child care services within a densely populated central urban area of some 320,000. At the time of the study it had no area office organisation. Its professional staff of about 50 child care officers and senior child care officers, organised into 8 area teams (or sectors) operated from 3 floors of a large office block. The building was shared with other tenants. Conditions in New Town were vastly different. The office was itself only a small part of the county children's department; one of eight such offices. A staff of 13 professional workers responsible for an area containing approximately 64,000 people, were operating from a large converted eighteenth-century dwelling house, occupied solely by the child care staff.

Each sector in Borough comprised two rooms: a small office occupied by a senior child care officer, and a much larger area with desks for up to seven or eight child care officers and a sector clerk. The premises in New Town allowed for each child care officer and senior child care officer to have his or her own room or, at most, to share with one other person. Difference between the agencies and in the size of population for which each was responsible, are reflected in the levels of bombardment faced by the two organisations.

LEVELS OF BOMBARDMENT

Over a two-week recording period in Borough, 829 clients called

F

at the reception office. Of these, as Table 2 shows, 539 were clients of the children's department. In New Town over a similar period of time the receptionist-telephonist dealt with a total of only 82 client visits (See Table 4 below). During the same two weeks almost 100 personal visits were made to the Borough office by *new* clients, compared with only 16 visiting New Town. In both cases the reception staff claimed that the weeks for which records were collected were no different in terms of client demand from any other two-week period. Although wide variations in bombardment from week-to-week did occur, especially in the office with a very low overall bombardment, this assessment appears to tally with the records in the 'visitors book' kept in each reception office.

Table 4

'KNOWN' AND 'UNKNOWN' CLIENTS AND CALLS[a] AT NEW TOWN OVER TWO WEEKS

	No. of Clients	% of Total	No. of Calls[a]	% of Total
Known	53	77	66	80
Unknown	16	23	16	20
Total over two weeks	69	100	82	100

[a] Includes revisits during study period.

The relatively low level of bombardment on the New Town office can largely be explained in terms of the nature of the agency, the size of the population for which it was responsible and very real differences in the incidence of need amongst the population. However, as has already been suggested, the staff of New Town conducted a very large part of their work either over the telephone or by personal visits to clients at home. This was made possible by the geographical compactness of the area, and good, relatively traffic-free, roads. In Borough mobility was rather more restricted by a road system and degree of congestion typical of the inner London area. Here the majority of child care officers tended to encourage their clients to visit them at the office. This practice itself increased an already high level of bombardment which, in turn, made it more difficult for child care officers to leave the office to see clients at home.

The variations in the type of agency and the levels of bombardment faced necessitated a very different arrangement of reception facilities in the two settings.

RECEPTION FACILITIES

The reception requirements of the New Town area office were far more limited than those provided in Borough. The office itself was a single-purpose building and the receptionist was therefore not faced with the problems of dual responsibility as in the Borough situation. The relatively small number of visitors to the building necessitated only one receptionist on duty at any one time, although in practice two were employed—one in the morning, one in the afternoon.

Facilities were arranged as follows. The main entrance to the building faced on to one of the main roads crossing the oldest part of the town and was clearly sign-posted externally as offices of the 'Children's Department'. A client on arrival entered the narrow passage behind the main door and was faced with a sign, indicating a door to the left, which read: 'Waiting-room: Please enter and inquire at the window'. Immediately on entering the waiting-room the client could see the receptionist-telephonist who was usually operating the switchboard, through a sliding glass window which separated the receptionist's room from the waiting area. Clients either waited at the window or sat on one of the chairs provided until the receptionist left her desk, slid back the window and spoke to them. For clients visiting the office, once the difficulties of geographical location had been overcome the physical barriers to access, in terms of finding the office, locating the reception-room and ambiguity in the reception situation itself, were minimal. The contrast with the difficulties faced by visitors to the Borough office was considerable.

The waiting-room was thoughtfully decorated with children's pictures, and furnished with a number of comfortable chairs and a table displaying magazines and comics. A selection of toys were stored in one corner to occupy waiting children. The room was rarely crowded; for the most part clients arrived and waited singly rather than in any number.

CLIENT RECEPTION PRACTICES

In spite of these considerable differences in the conditions under which they were working, the reception staff in New Town were subject to pressures similar to those in Borough to expand their role and become increasingly involved in interviewing, giving advice and advocacy. All of the reception practices described in detail in the Borough study were seen at one time or another in New Town. Both the morning and the afternoon receptionists operated in very much the same way. Clients were interviewed and their problems discussed; some were helped, others hindered in their attempts to see a social worker; advice and practical help was given. The major difference in the activities of reception staff in Borough and New Town was not what they did, but the frequency with which they did it. Although an initial reception interview was a fairly common feature of client reception in New Town, involvement beyond this stage was the exception rather than the rule. For Borough the reverse was true.

The likelihood of a receptionist in New Town undertaking an initial interview with a client, and the extent of any subsequent involvement, depended on whether or not the visitor was previously unknown or already known to the department. With *new clients* receptionist involvement occurred at least to the extent of discussing with the visitor their reasons for visiting the agency. This practice developed as a result of two basic tasks given to the reception staff as part of the agency's formal intake procedures. In the first place they were required to collect sufficient information from new clients to enable them to ensure that a client had arrived at the correct department for their needs. Second, they were responsible for making sure that all apparently 'new' clients were not already known to the department from a previous contact. As in Borough, in order to make these checks the receptionist was required to complete an 'Initial Inquiry Form' on the basis of the information given to her by the client. To perform both of these prescribed tasks the receptionist had no alternative but to ask clients about themselves and about their reasons for visiting the office—the basis of the reception interview. Once the process of interviewing had been initiated, continued involvement was obviously much more difficult to curtail than it would otherwise have been. The ways in which the agency's intake procedures produced pressures on reception staff to undertake an initial interview with new clients were described very succinctly by one child care officer as follows:

'Three years ago a client arrived, said who or what they wanted and were seen. Now receptionists complete the duty book[1] and a referral form; find out whether or not they've been before; write out messages for child care officers who aren't in. Generally they find out more about what the problem is than they used to. They *have* to.'

Receptionists also undertook an interview with some clients who were already known to a child care officer, although less frequently than for new clients. Much of the time the reception interview was omitted and the request for details about the reason for the visit, so common in Borough, was exceptional. In the majority of cases, contact between a visitor and a child care officer was achieved on the basis of information offered by the client at the point of reception. Receptionist involvement beyond this occurred primarily when the officer responsible for the case was for some reason unavailable. Under these circumstances the client would be asked to explain in brief the reason for the visit to enable the receptionist either to leave a message for the child care officer responsible, or to adjudicate on whether or not the case should be referred to the duty officer.

'You get some [clients] who can't wait to tell you their problems. . . . Usually if they can see someone I stop them [talking] and put them through to someone in authority. If they get started, especially if I know the child care officer isn't there, I usually let them go on and then I can tell the child care officer all about it when they get back. . . . I'm expected to write it up and leave a message in the "pigeon-holes" anyway. Then the child care officer can do something about it, if necessary, when they come in.'

Here the receptionist was very conscious of the willingness of many clients to explain in detail their reasons for coming to the agency to the first person they see. This was undoubtedly in part due to their desire (or need) to tell someone about their difficulties. But, in addition, problems were often described in an apparent attempt to impress upon the receptionist the urgency of the situation. Whether this was because of a belief on the part of some clients that the receptionist herself could provide them with the help they needed, or whether to persuade her to act as an intermediary on their behalf is unclear. The effect was the same—further

---

[1] The name and address of every visitor to the agency was entered into a 'visitors' book' kept by the receptionists as a check list.

pressure on the receptionist to become more involved with clients' problems.

Her comments also demonstrate that the tendency for receptionists to undertake an initial interview with certain visitors was enhanced by the indirect support given to the practice by a number of child care officers. Several had become accustomed to asking them for further information about a client in the office before conducting their own interview; many requested information in addition to that included in messages written about clients who had called in the officer's absence. In short, both receptionists were aware that they were generally expected to be able to provide details about visiting clients over and above those which they would collect as part of their more limited prescribed tasks. A few child care officers expected the receptionists to take on an even more 'active' role. One commented:

> 'The beauty of the present system is that receptionists are placed so that they can hear officers talking; they're involved with caseload returns, with putting notes from clients in the pigeon-holes and so on. [They] are able to become involved to a greater extent and as a result are able to take an active part in helping.'

An important additional reason why reception staff might be expected to extend their function was the obvious satisfaction which they derived from their interaction with the agency's clients, both visitors and telephone callers. Contact with visiting clients in particular, and the element of discretion which this kind of work offered, was described by each independently as being their major source of work satisfaction. In this respect their present jobs were compared favourably with their previous employment in the department purely as telephonists. One extended the comparison further to her former industrial experiences:

> 'There's no comparison between this job and one in industry. There it's just a question of finding out who they [clients] want and putting them through. Here you have to get more involved. They tell you their problems and you have to sort out what they want. It's much more personal ... more interesting, of course.'

The high degree of work satisfaction derived from their contacts with clients provided a further important incentive for the reception

staff to develop and extend that part of their work which they found
to be most rewarding.

DISCUSSION

Throughout this chapter I have been describing how, despite
considerable pressures on New Town reception staff to become
involved with clients as they had in Borough, the extent of involvement was extremely limited, both in the number of cases and in
scope. In order to understand this important difference in reception
practice we must return to the circumstances under which reception
was taking place.

Factors limiting receptionist involvement in New Town

Nature of the reception task Receptionists in the Borough office
were faced with the task of dealing with the clients of two departments—children's and health. This questioning of visitors was often
necessary in order to identify the department required. By comparison, the reception task in New Town was a simple operation,
and the need for such detailed questioning very much less. The
area office was a single-purpose building and its reception staff
were responsible solely for the clients of that one department. A
large and unambiguous sign outside the main entrance helped to
ensure that few visitors made an obvious error when entering the
building. As a result, both New Town receptionists generally
assumed that a visitor had arrived at the right building, unless a
specific request was made for another. The lack of ambiguity in the
reception process, therefore, greatly reduced the necessity for
receptionists to elicit additional information from visitors beyond
that offered on their arrival at the desk.

Difficulties in achieving social worker-client contacts One of the
major problems faced by reception staff in Borough was that of
contacting social workers when clients arrived to see them. Whenever a child care officer was difficult to trace, the receptionist was
under considerable pressure to become involved and provide the
client with alternative reception services of the kind described. In
New Town locating the whereabouts of social workers was very
much easier than in Borough. Indeed, the low level of receptionist-
client involvement in this office can largely be attributed to the

general accessibility of the child care staff. There were a number of reasons why this was so.

First, bombardment on the New Town office was about one-tenth of that experienced in Borough: child care officers in the larger agency, and duty officers in particular, faced with a fairly constant succession of visitors, were frequently not available for interviews. The tendency for officers to use informal rationing mechanisms to avoid having to see clients (such as failing to answer the internal telephone, and asking colleagues to tell clients they are not in the office) was increased the heavier the demand. Social workers in New Town, on the other hand, were never exposed to this kind of pressure from visitors. Here the relatively small number of clients visiting the office were less disruptive to social workers' scheduled work and, as a result, they were afforded a rather high degree of priority. Thus with far fewer people to interview, child care officers in New Town were both more willing and more likely to be available for interviews. These differences in practice are reflected in the high proportion of client-visits to the New Town office which resulted in a meeting with a social worker (78 per cent), and also in the length of waiting time experienced by clients of the two agencies.[1]

A further ramification of the relatively low level of bombardment in New Town was that when a child care officer was known by the receptionist to be in the building but did not answer the telephone, she had sufficient time to be able to 'ring round' the agency to find him. The sheer weight of numbers in Borough made it impossible for the reception staff to be so thorough for each individual client, although in special cases a client might be promoted in this way.

The second reason why social workers were relatively easy to trace and contact was the size and layout of the area office. The reception room was located in the centre of the building, next to the main entrance. It contained the pigeon-holes through which all the departmental post was distributed, and the main notice-board for the agency's staff. As a result, Reception was constantly frequented by social workers throughout the working day, and receptionists were able to maintain a fairly accurate knowledge of

[1] Fifty-four per cent of visitors to Borough waited for more than fifteen minutes before seeing a social worker, as opposed to only 26 per cent in New Town. In Borough 29 per cent waited for more than thirty minutes whereas only 5 per cent of visitors to New Town waited this long.

where particular officers were at any one time. Informal observations of this kind served to supplement the entries which social workers made about their future movements in the diary kept on the reception desk.

Alternatives to receptionist involvement

The New Town case shows that receptionist involvement can be reduced by making social workers more accessible for intake work. It also demonstrates the importance of ensuring that an agency's intake system contains readily available alternatives to involvement which provide reception staff with a more acceptable 'escape route' when faced with difficulties. For example, one important aspect of the intake procedure employed in New Town which limited the receptionists' role was the practice of accepting messages from visiting clients for absent social workers. A client whose child care officer was not available would generally be asked if they would like to leave a message. If the client agreed, the receptionist would write out a brief account of the client's reason for visiting. This was then pigeon-holed until the officer's return. Whilst this procedure inevitably resulted in the receptionist conducting a brief interview with the client, it may in itself have reduced the likelihood of further involvement. The client was able to see that something positive had been achieved as a result of her visit, and the receptionist had clearly demonstrated that she had done as much as she was able to do.

A second alternative to involvement was available in New Town. Each child care officer in the agency was assigned a member of the clerical staff (or, more frequently, two child care officers shared one clerk) who was specifically responsible for work on the cases of that officer or officers. It was accepted practice that if a client visiting the office was unable to see their own social worker, he or she could be asked if they would like to speak to the relevant clerk 'in case they can do something'. The existence of this option reduced the need for extensive contact between the client and the reception worker. Although the social worker's clerk may then have reacted in the same way as the receptionist in an office where this facility was not available (advocating, suppressing, advising and so on), this practice at least protected the receptionist from some of the pressures to become extensively involved.

Finally, I have already described how the central location of the reception office meant that it was in constant use by the social work staff. One side effect of this was that there was usually someone around to keep an eye on what was happening at the reception window. This helped to ensure that a duty officer or other social worker was generally available to provide advice or assistance should the receptionist require it. Even where no officer was in reception at the time that a difficult problem arose there were a number of alternatives open to the receptionist which removed the necessity for her to become involved and attempt to resolve the problem herself. When both the child care officer and the duty officer were not available, and a client did not wish to see the clerk, senior child care officers and the area children's officers were fairly easily accessible and willing to be called in. The lack of any facility of this kind in Borough was responsible for some of the more obvious encroachments by reception staff into tasks more usually associated with social workers.

Chapter 5

WEST COUNTY

The West County area children's office was responsible for the provision of child care services to a population of about 112,000 living in the borough and rural districts of West County. For much of the post-war period the staff of the office were accommodated in the premises of the local education division, but in 1966, following a series of protracted negotiations, the area child care staff were moved into a suite of rooms in the newly opened town hall. The space originally allocated to the children's department—at the time considered to be far from adequate—was still in use three years later at the time of this study, despite an increase of almost 100 per cent in staff during the intervening years.

The area office was situated on the second floor of the building and comprised seven rooms, including one interviewing room and a waiting area shared with the education department. Given the location of the officers amidst a maze of corridors within a much larger, multipurpose building, and the acute shortage of space for the child care staff, the reception requirements of the office were complex and the inherent problems difficult to overcome. The process of client reception to the department was essentially a two-part operation. First, a general receptionist situated inside the main entrance to the town hall was responsible for providing advice, information and directions to all visitors to the building who asked for assistance. Second, each department within the town hall had responsibility for its own arrangements for receiving callers directed to them by the receptionist on the ground floor. Clients of the children's department were met by the chief clerk (or, in her absence, by another available member of the clerical staff) on their entry into a partitioned-off area of the general clerical and typing-room.

The nature of the work and the problems faced by reception staff operating in these two, very different situations varied greatly. Each will be considered in turn.

RECEPTION TO THE TOWN HALL

Layout and barriers to access

The town hall, situated at one end of the main shopping centre for the town, was set back from the main road and was fronted by a wide paved area which gave the glass and pillored edifice a some- what forbidding appearance. All of the social workers interviewed commented upon the reluctance of many clients to approach the department because of the building's imposing facade. Inside, the general receptionist was located behind a large desk at one end of the entrance hall which served as foyer and waiting area for all visitors to the town hall.

In the original plans for the building, provision had been made for a 'direction indicator board' to be erected in the centre of the foyer facing the main entrance. A system of smaller directional signs had also been envisaged for strategic points such as the lifts and the stairs. This network of 'signposts' was, however, con- sidered to be a marginal cost at a time of general economic stringency and was never introduced. Thus visitors to the building relied almost entirely upon the directions given by the receptionist in the main hall to reach their destination. As a temporary measure, a cardboard sign had been attached to the wall just above the reception desk. But, as the receptionist claimed, only a small proportion of visitors understood it and the vast majority waited for confirmation from her or had to ask someone else. The inadequacy of this state of affairs was noted by the receptionist in a memorandum to the town clerk as early as April 1969. A brief extract from this document serves to indicate the kinds of difficulties faced by clients visiting one of the departments in the town hall:

'Many people do get lost in the building and tend to wander about due to the lack of notices on the other floors and I feel that the following notices should be installed to help the public:

ILLUMINATED LIFT SIGN (outside the lift doors)   This is necessary because the section of the corridor where the lift is located is dark and quite often when I direct people to the lift they don't see it. Instead they walk straight past and end up wandering along the public health department corridor.

SIGN WHICH SAYS
'INQUIRIES' ON MY
RECEPTION DESK

Numerous people wander through the main doors, look briefly right, and then left (towards the reception desk) and automatically turn right and ask the cashier at the borough treasurers reception for the information they require. The cashier then has to direct them back to me which wastes both her time and the customer's.'[1]

The receptionist's report continued in similar vein with additional detailed suggestions for signposting at strategic points and on the various staircases.

Difficulties of this kind faced by clients when first approaching one of the personal social service departments may seem trivial. For the timid, those uninitiated in the ways of bureaucracy and those for whom the decision to visit 'the Welfare' was a difficult one to make, the cumulative effect of these physical barriers to access is at the least unhelpful, at worst distressful and a possible restriction on further contact.

In 1971, five an a half years after the town hall had been opened, and two years after the memorandum had suggested improvements, signs were eventually erected throughout the building. The area children's officer was pleased that 'such an obvious deficiency' had been rectified. His one reservation was that the most direct and convenient route to the offices of the children's department was signposted "HOUSING".

Responsibilities of the ground floor receptionist

The general receptionist combined her reception duties with those of telephonist as in New Town. A switchboard identical to that in an adjacent switchboard room which was manned by a full-time telephonist was located in the centre of the reception desk. Thus, in periods of low bombardment at the desk the receptionist was able to act as telephonist and share the load of telephone calls. This method of combining receptionist and telephonist functions enabled the receptionist to concentrate her attentions upon inquirers at the desk when necessary, but to assist on the telephone

[1] 'Observations and Comments on the Notice Boards within the New Town Hall' (memorandum to the town clerk, 9 April 1969).

when the number of visitors subsided. At peak periods for visitors to the building the switchboard could be ignored and telephone calls were still received by the full-time operator.

As the person at the receptionist desk was not responsible for answering all telephone calls this enabled her, when necessary, to concentrate her attentions on visitors, thus removing a potential source of conflict of function which was occasionally apparent in the New Town setting. There, telephonist duties, including both incoming and outgoing calls, were given priority over clients waiting at the 'window', although total bombardment from visitors was sufficiently low for this potential difficulty to be accommodated with a minimum of dysfunctional consequences.

The primary task of the receptionist was to receive all callers at the building; to provide information, advice and assistance on request, and to direct visitors to the departments they required.[1] In common with other receptionists, she had been provided with no instructions as to what her responsibilities entailed, or how the task of receiving visitors should be performed. No attempt had been made, either at the time of her appointment or later to ensure that she was aware of interdepartmental divisions of responsibility. Thus, once again, senior and middle management appear to have assumed that the duties of a receptionist were self-evident, and that no instructions or training was relevant to the performance of the task. The receptionist herself noted this lack of direction and instruction: 'You just come and start doing what you have to. One thing follows on from the next. You have to use your own ingenuity. . . . I know the local area very well . . . and information about the different departments and services you just pick up as you go along.'

Similar comments on the 'self-evident' nature of the reception process were made by staff in each of the case-study offices. This common-sense element played a very important part in developing many of the reception practices described. For the general receptionist in the town hall, however, extension of the reception function was limited by certain negative controls imposed by the town clerk, and a range of standing instructions from individual departments as to how their clients should be treated. Both of these limitations had developed incrementally in response to problems as they arose.

[1] This brief summary of her duties is based on discussions with the receptionist herself and other members of staff, and observation during the study.

The former had arisen following complaints to the town clerk about a long waiting time at the desk, or of being disconnected during a telephone call. He had asked the receptionist on several occasions to explain the circumstances surrounding such incidents. As the receptionist herself put it, 'We've had a number of DON'TS but not many DOS.' This kind of reaction to the work undertaken by the receptionist inevitably influenced future practice, in the same way as 'feed back' from child care officers in Borough influenced the performance of the reception function there.[1] The feedback, however, operated in reverse. In Borough the reactions of individual social workers tended to induce the reception staff to become even more involved with clients than might otherwise have been the case, whereas in the town hall situation the influence of feedback was rather to curtail involvement.

Standing instructions from individual departments both provided the receptionist with guide lines as to how she should approach her work, and enabled departments to maintain some measure of control over the initial reception of their clients. Practices between departments varied but, for the most part, as each had its own reception area, the ground floor receptionist was expected merely to direct clients to the relevant room or floor. This had not always been the case. When the building was originally opened, following her previous practice in a much smaller office, the receptionist had contacted particular social workers and officials in the various departments to inform them of the arrival of a particular client at the desk, or of a telephone call. It was very quickly established—by requests and objections from departments and individuals—that this practice was not desirable. Thereafter her contact with individual officials in connections with clients was kept to a minimum. Telephone calls were usually transferred to each department's own secretariat; visitors were simply directed to the relevant reception area.

DISCUSSION

Before this part of the study was undertaken, it was hypothesised that a receptionist responsible for directing clients to a range of different departments would need to become involved with the detailed reasons for client applications. In Borough, the reception task of differentiating between clients for only two personal social

---

[1] Chapter 3, p. 63.

service departments was one important reason why the reception staff undertook an initial interview. A fairly detailed questioning particularly of new clients was necessary in order to establish which was the appropriate department. It seemed reasonable from this observation to hypothesise that a receptionist dealing with visitors to more than two departments would develop an even higher degree of involvement in order to perform a rather more complex regulating task.

However, despite the very general nature of her brief, the receptionist at the town hall desk became far less involved with visitors than was the case in either Borough or New Town. Unlike the reception staff in each of these offices, during the study she engaged in very few detailed discussions with any client about their reasons for visiting the agency. Contacts with visitors were brief, simple, and only rarely was any attempt made by the receptionist to elicit further information beyond that offered by the inquirer. This was unusual. Having already conducted the studies of Borough and New Town, I had come to expect 'supplementaries'.

The key to variations in practice between the Borough and West County entrance hall receptionists lies in a difference in their orientation. The receptionist in Borough, and in each of the other offices examined, were *service orientated*, that is, they were integrated into the intake procedures employed by the agencies concerned. Basically their responsibility was to establish contact between visiting clients and individual social workers in the organisations for which they worked. At least partly as a result of their prescribed tasks reception staff became increasingly involved with clients and with the work of their departments. The responsibilities of the receptionist in the entrance hall, on the other hand, were far more restricted in scope. The staff of the personal social service departments, in particular, had made it very clear from the outset that the receptionist was not responsible for contacting individual workers on behalf of visitors, but merely for directing them to one of a number of reception rooms elsewhere in the building. In this sense she could be described as a *non-service receptionist*, performing a very different kind of function to that documented elsewhere in the case-studies. This lack of integration into the intake process of one particular department meant that she was subjected to few of the pressures to extend her function that were generally experienced by service-orientated receptionists.

She was not, for example, required to complete an initial referral form in order to check the departmental files. This task had lead to involvement in three of the four offices. She was not asked for information about clients by child care officers, or exposed to critical feedback for failing to filter clients effectively. As she was only the first-stage receptionist, she received very little comment from individual departments about how she was performing her task. Possibly most important of all, as she was not responsible for achieving social worker-client contacts, she did not face the major reception problems of dealing with clients when the relevant social worker was unavailable. In all cases she just directed people to the department they asked for or the one she thought they wanted.

In the absence of discussion as to the reason for a client's visit, how was the receptionist able to perform this task? Much has been said in previous chapters about the difficulty of receiving clients who frequently are not sure themselves about which department or individual they wish to see. In these cases, without some form of discussion of client's problems, it would be impossible to direct visitors accurately to their destination. In this lies the answer to the apparent contradiction. Free from many of the pressures towards involvement faced by service-orientated receptionists, the receptionist in the town hall lobby was not as concerned with accuracy of referrals as were her service-orientated counterparts. Some of the people who arrived at the entrance hall reception desk stated the department they required (or believed they required) and were directed to this office by way of the lift or the stairs. No discussion ensued once a particular department had been mentioned. In Borough and New Town the service receptionists faced with such a request would have probed further to ensure that the visitor did indeed require the children's department and had not been misinformed.

Almost invariably the receptionist acted upon the information given by the client rather than by asking additional questions. Those who did not know exactly which department they wanted tended to state their problem in a general way which enabled the receptionist to act on the basis of certain 'key words' in their brief exposition. Even in these cases little discussion took place. Although the directions she gave on the basis of information surrendered by visitors occasionally resulted in a caller being sent to the wrong department, the 'second line' of receptionists in the departments themselves were able to re-refer those who were initially misdirected to the correct office.

G

RECEPTION IN THE WEST COUNTY
CHILDREN'S DEPARTMENT OFFICE

When the staff of the area children's office in West County moved to their new premises in the town hall, there was no discussion about the problems of client reception or the form which reception facilities should take. From the outset it was generally assumed that, subject to minor modifications made necessary by the physical layout of the building, visiting clients would be received as they had always been. Thus, until just before the present study, the reception of visitors to the children's department offices had been undertaken in the general clerical and typing room by the chief clerk or, in her absence, by another clerical officer. Clients who were required to wait were shown into an adjacent waiting-room (shared with the education department) until they could be seen by a child care officer or otherwise attended to.

These arrangements were considered by the chief clerk to be far from ideal. Clients were interviewed in an already overcrowded room amidst the noises associated with any typing-pool—the constant clatter of typewriters, incoming telephone calls and conversation. Visitors could be seen to be distressed by the noise and the lack of privacy:

'They'd come in the door and you'd see their look of shock as they came into the room full of people. . . . Others, you'd see them put their heads round the door and pull them back again quickly thinking they'd come to the wrong place. I used to have to run after people or call after them, so see what the wanted. I didn't like that . . . I've always thought that our reception arrangements were insufficient.'

The chief clerk made her reservations known to the area children's officer requesting that the latter should partition off a section of the general office as a reception area. The area children's officer agreed to make the suggested changes and towards the end of 1970, two years after the alteration had been proposed, a partition was erected (Figure 4). The distressing ambiguity of the reception arrangements before this change in layout was largely resolved by the partition. Clients entering the door marked 'Children's Department: all inquiries' were immediately faced with a counter above which was a sliding glass panel. The chief

clerk/receptionist was usually seated at her desk beyond this
window ready to attend to visitors.

It is interesting to note that before the chief clerk intervened,
neither the area children's officer nor the child care staff seemed to

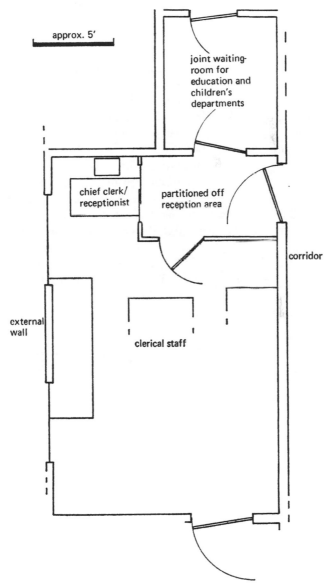

Figure 4   Reception Facilities at West County (Second Floor)

have recognised any inadequacy in the reception facilities provided, or, at least, had not made any dissatisfaction explicit. When the weaknesses were pointed out the area children's officer undertook to do what he could to resolve the problem, giving child care officers an opportunity to discuss the plans for the change at a staff meeting.

As in all of the case-studies reported so far, it was virtually impossible to establish the exact origins of particular reception procedures and practices. Many seemed to exist in their own right, no one remembering when they were introduced, by whom or, in many cases, why. The brief description of the reception process in West County which follows is derived from discussion with the receptionist herself and other members of staff, and from observations made during the study.

Procedures varied according to the 'known/unknown' status of the visitor. Once it had been established that a client had had no previous contact with the agency, the receptionist completed a 'Referral Slip'—a form requiring basic details about the client and his or her reasons for visiting the department. The client was then asked to wait in the waiting-room until called for. Details on the form were checked against departmental records to see if they contained any information about the client, the relevant child care officer was then informed and the client seen.

Where clients were already known to the agency, they usually arrived at the desk and asked to see a particular social worker. If the client had an appointment, he or she was asked to wait until the worker had been informed of their arrival. If no appointment had been made, the client was directed to the waiting-room and the whereabouts of the child care officer established. When an officer was for any reason unavailable for an interview, a visitor would be asked to call back, to 'telephone in', to leave a message or, under certain circumstances, would be given the option of seeing the duty officer.

As ever, a simple statement of the procedures followed when dealing with visitors to an agency provides very little insight into the real importance or impact of the functions performed by a receptionist, and, indeed, may obscure many of the most important features of her role. Some of these are discussed below.

PERFORMANCE OF THE RECEPTION FUNCTION

Despite considerable differences in the settings of Borough and

West County, reception staff performed very similar roles. Initial contact interviews, advocacy/suppression and the provision of reception services were common to both.

The development of an initial contact interview in West County is most easily understood by reference to the treatment of clients applying to the department for the first time. I have already described how the receptionist on the ground floor avoided involvement in the problems of individual clients. Thus, despite the two-stage reception process, the major responsibility for ascertaining whether or not a particular client had made a correct application to the children's department still rested upon the receptionist in the office itself. Quite apart from the chief clerks' own stated desire 'not to bother the child care staff unnecessarily', the area children's officer made his own expectations on this point quite explicit in discussion:

'Her job is to find out what the person's need is—that is, what their problem is—and as efficiently as possible to provide the next stage in the process, whatever that might be. This will involve referring them on to the right agency if they have obviously come to the wrong place, contacting the relevant child care officer, duty officer, or whatever.'

To perform this filtering task effectively, the receptionist was obliged to collect at least certain elementary details about the reasons for a client's visit, and this inevitably involved her in discussions about the client's problems.

An initial reception interview with new clients was also made necessary, as it had been in both Borough and New Town, by the requirement to complete the Referral Slip. This form was completed by the receptionist for all previously unknown clients calling at the office. In order to be able to, the receptionist had to ask the client a lot of questions about their background and their reasons for coming. In West County the information required included not only basic details such as the client's name, address and number of children, but also information on which children were involved in the application and the reasons for applying (e.g. 'Family Problem: State nature of problem', etc.).

In addition to these pressures, the chief clerk admitted to deriving a great deal of her work satisfaction from her contacts with clients and this increased the inherent tendency towards a high

level of receptionist involvement. New clients were rarely interviewed across the reception counter, but, when it was available,
they were taken by the receptionist into the nearby waiting-room.
This practice served the dual purpose of providing the client with
greater privacy in which to talk, whilst at the same time enabling
the receptionist to extend that part of her work from which she
gained most satisfaction—interviewing clients and discussing their
problems. The receptionist herself explained why she used the
waiting-room whenever possible: 'I think it helps one of my main
jobs which is to make people feel at home. I like making people
feel at home—it helps them to tell me their problems.'

In common with other offices, the initial interview was not
limited to the reception of unknown clients. Known clients were
interviewed particularly on those occasions when a visitor had
called to see an officer who was not available (by absence or
previous engagement), but also when the relevant child care officer
was in the office and not otherwise engaged. Each of these circumstances is discussed below.

When an officer was unavailable to see a visiting client, the
receptionist had the task of deciding which of a number of possible
courses of action to take. The client might be asked to leave a
message, which in itself involved the client in giving information
to the receptionist. Alternatively they might be asked to call back
or to telephone the office at a time when their child care officer
was more likely to be in. Or, thirdly, an interview might be
arranged with the duty officer for the day. In each of these cases
the decision as to which action was the most appropriate rested
with the receptionist herself. Both of these elements in the task,
gaining information and exercising discretion, were evident in the
receptionist's own description of her work:

'I like to try to make sure that the client is seen by the person
who eventually will be dealing with them. Otherwise they'd be
repeating their story three or four times. Every case is slightly
different. You have to make a decision for yourself. You have to
assess how urgent it is, and see what they *really* want. . . . If I
can steer them away from the duty officer, I do. If they're new
to the department I feel the duty officer should see them, but
not if they're already being seen by someone else. You get the
occasional one who gets a bit difficult or is particularly upset,
and you have to get the duty officer, but mostly you can deal

with it yourself by persuading them to come back later or to telephone in.'

By exercising her discretionary powers in this way, the receptionist can be seen to be potentially a very powerful buffer between clients and the social work staff. The nature of the intake practices of the agency enabled her to exercise a very high degree of discretion which to some extent determined whether a client would be seen, when and by whom. She was well aware of the extent to which she was able to exert influence and derived considerable satisfaction from this aspect of her work: 'Despite the fact that I'm chief clerk, most of my work is just routine and there's no chance for me to actually take decisions. Looking after reception enables me to take decisions'. Given these discretionary powers, the possibility of the further extension of the reception function to incorporate the provision of advice and guidance, advocacy/suppression and other 'reception services' was greatly enhanced.

The receptionist also acted as intermediary between client and social worker when the latter was in the office and available for interview. She regarded it as part of her task to provide each social worker with as much information about a visitor as she was able. To this end, rather than simply announce the arrival of a client over the telephone, she would frequently go to officers' rooms to inform them personally that a client wished to see them.

The layout of the office, together with this practice of telling each social worker personally of the arrival of a client, meant that I was faced with considerable practical difficulties in assessing the extent to which the receptionist extended her function to advocate, to suppress and to advise. However, in discussion many of the child care officers in the agency commented upon her practice of providing not only a detailed statement of the reasons for a client's visit (emphasising the importance of the initial interviewing function) but also, her tendency to provide her own assessment of the client's needs or difficulties.

One social worker believed that the type of reception received by a client was very much dependent upon how the receptionist reacted to their 'look':

'First impressions—formed from clothes, accent, personality— count for a lot. When she comes along from the waiting-room to announce the arrival of a client, she often gives her assessment of the client, together with a "run-down" on any other available information.

'If you're rather busy and therefore not feeling like being particularly energetic and she comes through the door, and says, "We've got Mrs —— in the waiting-room. I don't think it's particularly urgent. Do you want to see her or should I say you'll be in touch?" However much you try to counteract these pressures, this inevitably sets the scene and influences how you will react.'

Other child care officers expressed concern about the degree to which the receptionist's reaction to visitors influenced their own relationships with their clients:

'Sometimes [the receptionist] deals with problem herself and gives advice, and generally discusses the problem with them. . . . I would think that more often than not they are talked to and some impression given about what they ought to do. . . . And this is before they even see us. . . .'

Similarly:

'[The receptionist] knows too much about many clients and certainly has opinions about them—even new clients—and "sends out signals" which are bound to have some effect. Her attitude affects both the client's perception of us, and the way we react to them.'

Not all the child care staff were as critical as those already quoted of the degree of receptionist involvement with clients. Nevertheless, comments from other child care officers provide a further indication of the receptionist's potential influence.

'Mrs —— can make you job ten times easier by filling in on the background information about a client—especially if you haven't seen them before or your memory needs refreshing. It saves dragging back through the files and keeping the client waiting. . . .'

'I think [the receptionist] is very capable of sifting out people who don't really want the children's department. . . . She likes to make sure that we never see anyone unnecessarily, and is very thorough. We never see anyone unless we've first been told that they're here, and why.'

Whatever the opinions of the social work staff about the activities of the receptionist, and almost all of them made unsolicited reference to the high degree of involvement she maintained with visitors, the staff themselves did much to reinforce the interaction. The practice of the receptionist performing an initial interviewing function had developed in response to a number of elements in the reception situation. These have been described. It was enhanced and maintained by child care officers themselves who had come to expect the receptionist to provide them with information about waiting clients. This expectation, and requests for further details, reinforced the receptionist's tendency towards involvement. In order to be able to provide this information to social workers, whether unsolicited or on request, she continually became involved in questioning clients about their reasons for visiting the agency. In relaying this information to the officer concerned her own attitudes to particular clients frequently became apparent.

In addition, both the receptionist and the clerical staff responsible for answering the telephone saw their role as protecting child care officers from 'unnecessary callers'. This was because in the past child care staff had made it clear that they might not wish to see, or speak to, particular clients should they contact the agency. As a result of these quasi-official instructions, no telephone call from a client was ever put directly through to a social worker without the telephonist-clerk first checking that he or she wished to speak to the client. Similarly, no visitor to the office was directed to a child care officer, or even told whether or not they were available, until the officer in question had been informed of the visit. The operation of this buffer process in the case of incoming telephone calls was explained by one of the clerks. It applies equally well to the reaction to clients visiting the office.

> 'If the caller is "an agency", the call is usually transferred straight through to the child care officer required ... if they are available. If it's a client it's much more difficult. You've never got to commit yourself. ... You must be non-committal. You never know whether a particular child care officer wants to talk to the client or not. You find out what they want, tell the child care officer and then they can decide. Occasionally they're not in. Some child care officers get very annoyed if you say they're in without checking with them first.'

In both of these ways, by requesting information and by being

critical of the clerical staff when they failed to act as an efficient
filter, child care officers in the agency required their clerical staff
and, in particular, the receptionist to become involved with
visiting clients.

Little need be said in this section to clarify or further expand upon
the reception processes identified in the West County office.
Readers will have noticed that despite great differences in the
conditions under which reception staff in Borough and West
County were operating, the process of client reception and the
activities of reception staff had developed along very similar lines.

It could be argued very simply that the development of these
aspects of the reception function in the West County office was due
primarily to the receptionist herself merely extending her
responsibilities in the direction which gave her the greatest amount
of personal work satisfaction. This was undoubtedly partly the
case: she admitted finding it difficult to resist becoming more
involved with clients than she already was because she enjoyed that
part of her work so much. Sadly, it was not possible within the
limitations of the present study, to attempt to measure the influence
of personality factors as a possible explanation for extension and
modification of the reception function. Both structural and
personality factors undoubtedly contributed to this process and
without a very complicated additional study no systematic attempt
could be made to measure their relative importance. At a subjective
level, however, there would appear to be strong evidence that
structural features far outweighed personality as a determinant of
the role of reception staff. The study of the Borough office provided
an opportunity to compare the role of different reception workers
operating under exactly the same conditions. In New Town two
receptionists shared the reception work—one in the morning and
one in the afternoon. In both cases, despite obvious personality
differences between the individuals concerned, the reception
activities they performed were remarkably similar. This comparison
was most striking in Borough. Here, two receptionists worked
concurrently. One was extremely jovial and extrovert and, like the
chief clerk in West County, said how much she enjoyed interacting
with visiting clients. Her colleague was rather timid, introverted
and reserved. Yet both of these receptionists played an equal part
in modifying the basic reception function as described. As has been

argued throughout the analysis, structural features in the reception situation played a very large part in determining the nature of the reception process. These pressures towards receptionist-client involvement were similar in the West County office and appeared to outweigh personality factors in explaining the chief clerk's role.

A final comment should be made about the structure of reception in the West County town hall. Before undertaking this case-study, I had expected to find a number of features peculiar to this two-stage arrangement. The reception process at the main entrance was indeed very different from that which was developed by service-orientated reception workers. But the activities of the chief clerk in the children's department suite were not significantly different from those in any of the offices which did not have the 'benefit' of an initial screening. This was undoubtedly due to the very minimal role played by the receptionist at the main entrance. She was concerned with directing people to a range of offices and not with ensuring the 'appropriateness' of a visit or for establishing contact with an individual social worker. These tasks still had to be done by the service receptionist in the offices themselves. Thus, whilst the two-part reception process may have been somewhat confusing to visitors, especially to those re-referred at stage two, it appeared to have little influence on the department's own intake process.

Chapter 6

CASSFORD

Earlier case-studies have provided examples of degrees of receptionist involvement with clients at the point of intake and the effect of this on the decision-making process as to who should receive what services, when, and from whom. Despite variations in the extent to which this influence was exerted, some degree of receptionist-client involvement and the provision of reception services occurred in every case. This final study is of a client reception process in which the role of the receptionist was subtly different from those described above. In Cassford, involvement with clients was virtually non-existent, and any extension of the reception function beyond the basic elements of the receptionist's tasks as formally prescribed was very rare indeed. This variation is explained largely in terms of the absence in Cassford of the structural pressures towards involvement and task ascription which were so much in evidence in each of the other offices.

THE DEVELOPMENT OF FACILITIES

The offices occupied by the children's department in Cassford were purpose-built in 1961–2. The staff operating from this building were responsible for a total population of some 185,000 people in the town of Cassford and its surrounding districts. Originally the building had been intended to accommodate about twenty to twenty-five professional and clerical staff. By February 1964, following the appointment of additional staff, the area children's officer considered the buildings to be far from adequate, and was making representations to the divisional education officer (responsible for all negotiations with the county council about staffing, office space and the like) to the effect that 'Parkinson's Law is already beginning to operate and we are bursting at the seams in our new offices'.[1]

[1] Communication to Divisional Education Officer, February 1964.

Conversion and extension of the building began in 1965 and was to proceed in a number of stages. Provisional plans for the largest and most recent alteration, the addition of 1,330 square feet of floor space, were drawn up by the county architect in March 1967 and copies submitted to the children's department and the area officer for consideration. The area officer, following consultations with his staff, suggested a number of alterations to the proposals to make the best possible use of the increased floor space, and to provide more suitable facilities for dealing with visitors. Discussions followed between May 1967 and July 1968 when the area children's officer's amendments were accepted and incorporated into a revised plan.

In the original architect's drawing for the new extension, the entrance had been at the rear of the building and not visible from either the road or the driveway. The new plan, based on the advice and comments of the social work staff, placed the main entrance to the office in a more 'obvious' position, far more easily accessible to visitors. As a result, after the alterations, the main entrance was located at the side of the office.

This move had been made in an attempt to improve client access to the building, but it was rather undermined by the system of signposting used. A small black and white notice on the front wall of the building read: 'Area Children's Office'. Adjacent to this, many times larger and in red lettering on a white background, a second sign bore the apparently contradictory statement: 'EDUCATION DEPARTMENT ONLY'. This latter sign referred to the car park of the adjacent building but confusion could be excused. This undoubtedly accounted for the fact that over 10 per cent of callers at the Cassford children's department office during the recording period wanted the education department.

In addition to other modifications, the new plan provided for a slightly larger waiting area and a toilet for visiting clients, more adequate interviewing rooms adjacent to the waiting room; and the receptionist-telephonist was located in a room next to the main entrance and connected to it by a small glass window. An alcove was constructed around this 'inquiries hatch' to separate clients in the waiting room from those speaking to the receptionist. The hatch was also accoustically treated with sound proofing panels.

DUTIES OF THE RECEPTIONIST

The receptionist combined her responsibilities for receiving

visiting clients with that of manning the office's telephone switchboard. Figure 5 shows her location in relation to the main entrance.
Clients entering the lobby were faced with a sign asking them to
'PLEASE RING AND WAIT', and were spoken to through the inquiries
hatch.

A major feature of the receptionists' role in the other case-studies
was the lack of any detailed statement of their duties and responsibilities. Reception procedures were generally ill-defined and, by
default, permitted a very high level of discretion to the reception
staff as to how to deal with individual clients. In addition, where
some form of official definition of the receptionists' duties did
exist, it was seen to be frequently inappropriate to the actual
conditions faced by the reception staff at the desk. These two
features of the reception process, together with pressures from the
social workers themselves, produced variations in and extensions
of the basic client-reception function.

The situation in Cassford was very different. First, the intake
procedures employed in the office were clearly defined, and within
this framework the limits of the receptionist's responsibility were
formally and explicitly delineated. Second, and more important,
the tasks prescribed to the receptionist were appropriate to her
operating situation and, as a result, the pressures towards the
modification of functions were minimised. These features of the
client reception process in Cassford can be seen to have had an
important influence upon how clients were received to that office.

The area children's officer on her appointment in 1968, had been
faced with what she described as 'an extremely unstable and
unstructured situation'. Many of the more senior staff in the office
had, like herself, only recently been appointed and were unclear
as to their own spheres of responsibility and to the specific needs of
the area. The level of client bombardment on the office at the time
was also particularly high for the child care staff available. As the
area children's officer explained, 'this nightmare period necessitated
a constant reappraisal of procedures just to get the work
manageable'.

In response to discussions initiated by the area officer and
senior child care officers, various procedures for dealing with
different kinds of cases were formalised and written up as instruction
sheets. As part of this process the procedures to be followed by the
receptionist-telephonist when dealing with visitors and telephone
calls were also detailed. These receptionist tasks were as follows.

All clients, with the exception of the few 'regulars' who would be immediately recognised by the receptionist, were asked for their name and address, and whether or not they had been to the office before. *They were then asked to wait in the adjacent waiting-room.* If a client said that he or she had had no previous contact

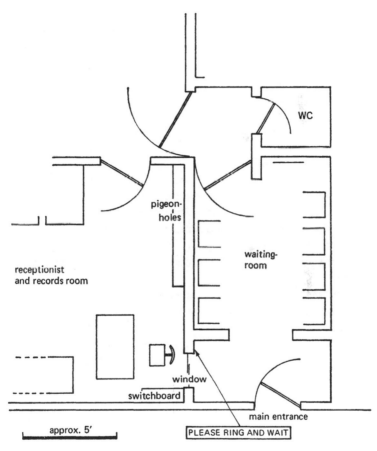

pigeon-holes

WC

waiting-room

receptionist and records room

window

switchboard

main entrance

approx. 5'

PLEASE RING AND WAIT

Figure 5   Reception Facilities at Cassford

with the department, the records (located in the reception-room) were checked for existing information. The duty officer was telephoned and asked to see a new client. This social worker was then given the client's name and address, plus any 'papers' which might have been found. The client was collected from the waiting area by the social worker and taken to one of the interviewing rooms. During this initial intake interview the duty officer completed a New Referral Form.

The procedure for a client who was already known to an officer in the agency was equally straightforward. If the relevant social worker was in the building and available to see a visitor, the receptionist informed him of the client's arrival. The client was then collected from the waiting-room by the social worker, and accompanied to an interviewing room. If a child care officer did not appear to collect a client, a subsequent 'reminder' telephone call was made.

When the required social worker was not available, the client was told of the officer's absence and automatically given the option of seeing the relevant clerk or the duty officer. If neither of these was available (an unusual occurrence), or the client did not wish to speak to the clerk, a senior child care officer or the area children's officer could be informed.

Perhaps, surprisingly, the reception and intake practices of reception staff in Cassford corresponded very closely with this brief outline of her formal duties. Involvement with clients beyond this minimum interaction was almost non-existent. This variation from the pattern described in earlier case-studies is explainable in terms of a number of features of the Cassford situation which were unique.

First, the receptionist was expected to put all new clients in touch with a social worker unless it was immediately obvious from the client's opening remarks that they had come to the wrong building. This helped to remove the necessity experienced elsewhere for the receptionist to probe for details about the reasons for the client's visit.

Almost inevitably, any new client arriving at a reception desk when applying for the assistance of an organisation will make some brief statement about their reason for visiting. Given the additional intake responsibilities of the reception staff in the first three offices described, this was followed up by these receptionists with 'supplementaries'—further questions to clarify the client's status *vis à vis* the agency, their reason for visiting and the urgency of their inquiry. The Cassford receptionist, on the other hand did not become involved with the clients-in-contact even to this extent. A client's brief account of the reasons for applying were usually passed on verbatim to the social worker on the telephone, and comments limited to the information volunteered by the client.

This could be seen from the content of the verbal messages given to child care officers when they were informed of a client's presence in the waiting room—'Mrs —— to see you from —— Road. She wants some more information on fostering', or 'A Mr —— is in the waiting-room. He's having trouble with his son and wants to talk to someone about it'. Messages of this kind when passed on by the receptionist were almost invariably couched in the actual words which had been used by the client. Such volunteered information was sufficient to enable the receptionist at Cassford to perform her limited prescribed responsibilities. On this basis she was easily able to ascertain that a visitor did indeed require a social work department and not the nearby education office. As has already been noted, the signposting layout outside the building produced some confusion for visitors as to which building belonged to which department. This resulted in a fairly high proportion of visitors, who really required the education department, approaching the child care reception desk. In virtually all of these cases, however, the error became apparent during the brief client-receptionist contact—the client asking either for someone employed in the education office or asking to see an 'education officer'. All other visitors were passed on to the duty officer or clerk in the usual way. No further probing by the receptionist to ensure an appropriate approach to the agency was considered necessary, or proved to be so.

This procedure has the added advantage that the receptionist was not exposed to the negative feedback of social work staff when she failed to filter accurately or to provide additional information before conducting their own interview. They simply did not expect her to perform this kind of role, and modified their own responses accordingly.

The second reason for low involvement was that the receptionist was not required to complete any kind of initial inquiry form. The only information she was responsible for collecting from visitors was their name and address, and their own statement as to whether or not they had had dealings with the children's department before. The case was then passed on to the duty officer who undertook the preliminary interview and completed the necessary paperwork. It was at this stage in the process that decisions were made about whether or not a client should be referred on to another agency, what kind of assistance might be appropriate or whatever.

It is worth noting that, towards the end of the study, the
H

receptionist and her colleague were informed of the initial inquiry practices observed in each of the previous studies. They were genuinely astonished to learn that their own procedure in dealing with new clients was, in my experience, unusual, and that elsewhere receptionists were required to collect initial basic data from new applicants. The receptionist commented:

'I couldn't do that. Occasionally people won't even give me their address, let alone tell me anything else. You can't complete a Referral Form if you're not going to get involved with the case. Apart from anything else you'd not get enough information. . . . It would take ages and the [switch] board would get chocker.'

A third key feature of the intake process in Cassford concerned the procedures detailed for dealing with known clients. The problems generated for receptionists by social worker inaccessibility have been discussed at length in other case studies. Uniquely amongst the agencies visited, this created no major difficulties for the staff of the Cassford office. Here alone, the procedure to be followed by the receptionist in the absence of a social worker was made explicit and covered all conceivable variations in circumstances.

When a client had given 'her' name and address and was seated in the waiting area, the receptionist's first call was to the relevant social worker. This was to either the duty officer or the social worker to whom the case had been allocated. If this child care officer was not in the building or not available, the client was given the option of seeing the officer's clerk or the duty officer. If neither of these were available, or if the client did not wish to see one or other of them, the receptionist could call upon a senior child care officer or, in the last resort, the area children's officer. In practice, the majority of clients in this situation were prepared to speak to their own social worker's clerk who would then be able to take a message and/or inform the client about the child care officer's likely movement in the near future.

The practice of involving child care officers' clerical assistants directly in dealing with visiting clients in Cassford resulted in only a very small proportion of visitors to the agency not being seen by someone other than the receptionist. In Cassford only 5 per cent of all visitors during the recording period were seen only by the receptionist, as opposed to 16 per cent in New Town, 24 per cent in Borough and 27 per cent in West County.

As was noted in connection with a similar practice in New Town, the involvement of clerks in the reception and intake process was inevitably open to many of the same kind of 'abuses' and clerical involvement in the sphere of the professional worker as have been recorded when receptionists themselves perform this task. However, the practice enabled the receptionist at least to avoid the difficulties which normally result from social work staff not being available.

The problem of inaccessibility in Borough and elsewhere was exaggerated by child care officers' unwillingness to be interrupted during their supervision sessions, meetings and so on even when they were in the building. In Cassford the position on this had been clarified by the relevant instruction sheet issued by the area children's officer following consultations with her staff on procedure.

'The telephonist-receptionist to contact officers, even if they are at a meeting, the officer then to decide whether to take the call or decide how it is to be dealt with. Duty officers who are at a meeting must either take the duty call or have arranged previously with someone else to do their duty work.

'When an officer, other than a duty officer, is interviewing and does not wish to be interrupted, the telephonist-receptionist will put a call through to the duty officer or clerk, and duty officers will be told when they have another client waiting.

'The telephonist-receptionist to be told when meetings are taking place so that she will know where to find officers. Only very exceptionally will there be a meeting which is not to be interrupted.'

Each of these instructions clarified the procedure to be followed for callers and removed the onus of responsibility for decision-making in each case from the receptionist herself.

The receptionist's task of locating social workers was undoubtedly made easier in Cassford by a further factor, and one which is much more difficult for practitioners to control. The West County office was dealing with an average of about fifty-three visitors each week and had a staff of thirteen social workers; Cassford, faced with roughly the same bombardment rate, had a social work staff of thirty. Such anomalies still exist in social service departments and are bound to remain until the criteria for area office staffing are related to relevant indicators of need in the areas concerned.

The Cassford office provides an example of the reception function being performed with a minimum of receptionist influence on the day-to-day operations of the agency. This was achieved (not altogether intentionally) by the establishment of an intake process which exerted very little pressure on receptionists to become involved with clients, and by the close definition of intake procedures which had the effect of limiting the extent of the receptionist's discretion. The job was reduced to its bare elements, and the tasks involved could be performed quite adequately without elaboration or extension.

This analysis requires some further explanation in the light of the findings in the other case-studies. In each of the other offices, although in varying degrees, the reception staff extended their basic responsibilities in the direction of greater involvement with clients. A number of reasons for this phenomenon have been put forward, including the nature of the tasks prescribed to the receptionists. In the Cassford context, I have been arguing, the detailed specification of reception procedures by the area children's officer obviated the need for the receptionist to extend her function. But, in other offices described, even where procedures were clearly defined, they were modified by the reception staff in performing their work. Why in Cassford, should the definition of procedures be accepted by the receptionist where elsewhere they were bypassed, modified or completely ignored?

The number of variables in such an equation are considerable. Possibly the crucial factor was the personality of the receptionist and the area children's officer who outlined the procedures to be followed. But the consistency of practice in the first three offices despite obvious personality differences between the participants makes this unlikely. It might have been due to the fact that intake procedures were clearly defined and prescribed. But it is unlikely that the introduction of formal procedures would have greatly modified the reception practices in Borough, for example. The important difference appears to be not that procedures existed, but that in Cassford they were *appropriate* to the circumstances in which the receptionist was operating. In short, it was possible for her to remain within the limits of her defined power and still perform the tasks which other staff in the agency and clients expected her to perform.

Variations in the amount of discretion exercised by reception staff in different settings is a fascinating area for study and one worthy of more detailed examination than is possible here. But one observation must be made about receptionist discretion, particularly in view of the practical suggestions about dealing with the issue of reception power which are made in the next chapter. Blau refers to the importance of discretion amongst the reception clerks in the employment exchange.

'The exercise of discretion enabled the receptionist to derive satisfaction from helping people. It also made dealing with aggressive clients even less difficult, since it provided receptionists, who could refuse such a client a special consideration, with sanctions to discourage aggressive behaviour and to release their emotional reaction when it occurred. The clerk who exercised least discretion found conflicts with clients so irritating that he alone preferred other duties to those at the reception desk.'[1]

This paragraph could easily have been written to describe the reactions of reception staff in the present study. The major source of job satisfaction of receptionists in Borough, New Town and Cassford was their contact with visitors and derived from helping them to resolve their problems. For reception staff in Borough, in particular, the tasks they were expected to perform would not only have been less satisfying but virtually impossible had they been unable to exercise the discretion necessary to regulate the flow of clients to the office and to counter criticism or aggression. In New Town a wide element of discretion made a fairly routine job very much more interesting. The Cassford receptionist was unique in that she alone preferred her other duties—especially operating the switchboard—to dealing directly with visitors. Of all those interviewed, the receptionist in Cassford exercised by far the least amount of discretion—indeed her contact with clients had been kept to an absolute minimum. However, unlike Blau's interviewers, her preference for duties other than client reception was not primarily due to the difficulties she experienced when dealing with visiting

[1] Blau, P. M., *The Dynamics of Bureaucracy: A Study of Interpersonal Relations in Two Agencies* (Chicago University Press, revised edn, 1963), p.87.

clients. Most of the structural causes of receptionist-client conflicts had been removed in the planning of the intake procedures,
so that, at the very least, she was able quickly and easily to pass on
difficult clients to someone else in the organisation. Rather, her
low level of satisfaction with reception work resulted from the
lack of interest and variety that the absence of discretion produced.

This relationship between limited discretion and low job
satisfaction produces a paradox which must be tackled by anyone
concerned about the extent of receptionist influence. If a receptionist
is deprived of discretion in her treatment of clients, the job satisfaction she gains from this part of her work is likely to be reduced.
If such a reduction occurs, it seems likely that she will develop
compensatory satisfaction in other areas which in turn may impair
the effective performance of the reception function. Yet to increase
her discretionary powers is to run the risk of extending her
influence over important decisions relating to clients.

There is no simple solution to this problem. With careful
planning it should be possible to devise a system of client intake
which limits the discretionary power of the receptionist in those
parts of her work which involve crucial decisions, and allow the
development of discretion in other areas less significant for clients.
This was automatically done to some extent by the Cassford
receptionist who developed that part of her reception work which
was internal to the agency, and which ensured the smooth working
of procedures as laid down. For example, she was prepared
frequently to 'go upstairs' to find a particular child care officer
rather than to use the internal telephone. This was not accounted
for in the description of her responsibilities but was only a minor
modification of these in the interest of achieving the objectives of
her task as specified. In addition, the process of tracing an officer
in this way provided an important source of variation and interest
to an occupation which allowed only a minimum of personal choice.

Chapter 7

CLIENT RECEPTION
AND INTAKE

In the preceding chapters I have attempted to demonstrate the potential importance of the client reception process in a social service agency, and to identify the impact of receptionists' activities on the provision of primary agency services. The purpose of this final chapter is to summarise some of the main findings, to draw together a few loose ends and to highlight a number of practical implications of the study for those working in the social services. Whilst the fieldwork for this book was undertaken in children's departments, the findings are equally relevant to post-reorganisation social service departments. Perhaps even more so now that the organisations concerned are so much larger and more powerful.

ATTITUDES TO RECEPTION

The receptionist is usually regarded as a necessary and important member of an agency's staff, but is rarely thought to exert any direct impact upon the agency's primary tasks or objectives. This was the assumption made about the activities of the reception staff in almost all of the agencies contacted during the study, including many cases not reported in detail. This attitude was reflected in the ways in which reception offices had been established. The facilities available were usually a result not of conscious choice and planning but of chance, after other important decisions about room allocation and office layout had been made. In some cases the organisation of the reception office was not seen as an area of professional concern at all and was left entirely to an administrative section or O and M to arrange.

Attitudes towards the reception process are also demonstrated by the fact that in almost all the departments visited there was no official statement of the duties and functions of the receptionist, or of the role of reception within the agency's intake process. None of the reception staff had received any instruction or training for their work. Principles, procedures and techniques were simply passed on by existing staff to any new recruit by word of mouth.

The lack of any clearly communicated statement of responsibilities or tasks from an administrative or supervisory source resulted in the work of receptionists being based almost entirely on informal codes of practice. They were modified in an *ad hoc* way by other agency staff in response to particular events as they occurred, but for the most part the client reception process was dependent on the receptionists' own judgement and 'common sense' when deciding what to do in particular situations. The importance of client reception was almost universally undervalued.

RECEPTION FACILITIES

The conditions in which clients were expected to wait in the case-study offices were clean and tidy but generally ill-equipped and unwelcoming. In three of the offices, no toys were provided for waiting children, and in one of these the only toilet near to the reception office was designated 'STAFF ONLY'. In another, the air outlet from the specially built visitors' toilet had been constructed to flow into the waiting-room. This made an otherwise pleasant waiting-room a rather undesirable place to be.

Whilst something could be done to reduce the feelings of stigma experienced by someone approaching a social service department by providing an extra coat of paint for a waiting-room a comfortable chair or the odd piece of carpet, these deficiencies were not the most problematic element of reception facilities in the case-study offices. Far more important, in my view, was the general lack of privacy for visitors when explaining to the receptionist their reasons for visiting the office. Time and time again, as I sat in a variety of waiting-rooms, I saw obvious distress on the part of visiting clients who were obliged to describe their problems in a room containing other people. The receptionists, accustomed to tales of misery and deprivation, were hardened to most of the stories they were told and failed to see the lack of privacy as a problem. This was obvious from their attitude to visitors, and from the way in which clients were asked to 'speak up' when they had obviously been trying to retain an element of intimacy between themselves and the receptionist.

Two of the case-study offices had made a conscious attempt to deal with this problem. In Cassford, sound-proofing had been erected around the inquiries hatch, and this itself was situated some distance away from the waiting area. The West County chief clerk had arranged for a partition to be built to separate off an area of the main office for reception purposes. A third office, not included in the case studies, had arrived at an even more satisfactory solution. In addition to separating the waiting-room entirely from the reception desk, the staff had placed a notice on the desk which read: 'If your inquiry is confidential, please say so and you will be seen in private.'

THE ROLE OF THE RECEPTIONIST

Detailed examination of the activities of reception staff in the four offices demonstrates the potential importance of the reception function in any service agency—particularly one concerned with social services. Here my intention is to identify some of the common features of reception practice and to suggest reasons for their development.

The first interview
In three of the studies, service-orientated receptionists were frequently involved in conducting an initial contact interview with visitors to the reception office. The depth and frequency of this interview varied but in each case it involved eliciting from the caller the reason for their visit and a more or less detailed discussion of clients' problems. The Cassford office was something of an exception in that the initial contact interview by the receptionist had been consciously avoided by the introduction of an intake procedure which made it unnecessary. The account which follows is drawn primarily from the analyses of Borough, New Town and West County.

As the visitors' first point of contact with the agency, the receptionist was given the task of greeting new arrivals and ensuring that they had come to the right place. In the context of a pre-Seebohm social service agency, this task was not as simple and straightforward as it might at first appear. This difficulty was noted in the Seebohm committee report itself:

'Many of those submitting evidence stressed the difficulty

which the public and members of other services found in approaching the local authority personal social services. People are often unclear about the pattern of services and uncertain about the division of responsibilities between them. Initially a person's true need (sometimes a matter for expert diagnosis) may not be clearly recognised; sometimes the person seeking help may be confused or inarticulate and unable to make plain what particular help he requires. In such circumstances it may be difficult for him to get straight to the right services and the delay and further referral this involves may be dicouraging, particularly if the local offices of different services are a considerable distance apart.'[1]

As this comment suggests, 'the Council', 'the Welfare', 'the Social Security' are frequently undifferentiated by many clients and potential clients of the personal social services, and this may cause confusion when the need arises for contact. Any applicant may easily select the wrong agency to deal with their particular problem or inquiry. There is evidence to suggest that even those who work within one arm of the social service system have a very incomplete knowledge of the activities and responsibilities of other social welfare agencies.[2]

For new applicants to the children's departments in the case studies, therefore, the receptionist was not able without some discussion with the visitor to decide on the relevance or otherwise of an application. She had little option but to listen to the clients' account of their problems and on this basis decide whether or not this was the responsible agency. Given the way in which the service-orientated receptionists perceived their task, this could rarely be achieved on the basis of the clients' initial statement and frequently necessitated supplementary questioning and probing by the receptionist.

Even where a visitor requested a department or individual social worker by name the receptionists questioned further. By experience they knew that new applicants had frequently been misinformed, or had made incorrect assumptions about the split of departmental responsibilities. A social worker's name might have been given by a

[1] *Report of the Committee on Local Authority and Allied Personal Social Services* (HMSO, 1968), Cmnd 3703, para 83.

[2] 'Feeling the Pulse' (survey by the Queen's Institute of District Nursing); Anderson, J. A. D. and Warren, E. A., 'Communications with General Practitioners', *The Medical Officer* (1966), Vol. 118, No. 3.

friend, or have been remembered from a previous contact with the department months, or even years, before.

The need to undertake in some cases a fairly detailed interview with new applicants was reinforced in Borough, New Town and West County by the agencies' intake procedures. In each case reception staff were required to complete an initial inquiry form (variously named) at the point of first contact for every visitor identified as a new applicant. The forms varied in the amount of detail they required, but all requested basic information such as the client's name; address; number, names and ages of children; and a summary of the reasons for their visit. In one case the standard form required further information on occupation, religion of parents, place of employment and such like.

The use of the initial inquiry form had two main effects on the reception process. In the first place, it made it impossible for the receptionists to undertake their prescribed tasks without a sufficiently detailed interview to enable them to complete the form. Second, the existence of the form was seen as a formal approval of reception interviews. A number of receptionists were thus encouraged to develop and expand that area of their work from which they gained most satisfaction—interviewing clients, discussing and commenting upon their problems.

Reception staff in each of the offices were faced with a series of additional pressures upon them to become increasingly involved in the details of clients' problems and inquiries. Whilst these were only described in detail in the Borough study, they were clearly in evidence elsewhere. For example, social workers themselves frequently asked receptionists for further information about a particular waiting client before undertaking their own interview. Queries of this kind made it imperative for receptionists to be able to meet such requests when they were made. Conversely, negative feedback from a social worker about a client who had been 'wrongly' referred through to them increased receptionists' resolve to be more effective in future.

So far specific reference has been made only to initial contact interviews with new clients approaching the agency for the first time. In two of the case-studies, interviews of this kind were also fairly common when dealing with clients who were already on the caseload of a social worker. In New Town they occurred, but less frequently. The main occasion when reception interviews involved current case clients was when a client's social worker was from some

reason not available or could not be found. In each case the receptionist was given the task of adjudicating upon the urgency or
otherwise of an inquiry. If it was considered sufficiently urgent,
the duty officer could be contacted. If not, the client was asked to
call back or to leave a message. In order to establish the degree of
urgency, the receptionist needed sufficient information about the
details of the problem in order to reach an assessment, and again a
probing interview was a necessary part of the process.

Reception services

In addition to the initial reception interview, there were a variety
of other ways in which reception staff were seen to impinge upon
areas of professional discretion and responsibility. They provided
clients with a range of positive reception services.

Some of these quasi-professional activities developed directly
out of the initial contact interview. In the case of new clients in
particular, receptionists became involved in deciding not only
which department they required but also for which service they
ought to apply. The example given in the text was of one reception
worker deciding whether or not reception into care or a day
nursery placement was the most appropriate service in particular
cases and making a referral accordingly. There were many others.
In these cases some of the more important decisions in relation to
the client's application had been taken before a social worker had
been contracted. This help given by the receptionists, especially
to new applicants, in formulating their service request was an
important reception service—a service which would rank amongst
those normally associated with professional social workers.

Possibly the most common reception service was the ability and
willingness of receptionists to act as advocates on behalf of clients
in their contacts with the social work staff. Receptionists were
expected to inform child care officers that clients were waiting to
see them. When a client was not seen quickly, however, the
receptionist would frequently make further telephone calls (often
stressing urgency) to ensure that the client was eventually seen
and as quickly as possible. Subsequent calls might be made directly,
as a simple reminder, or indirectly on the pretext of foregetfulness.
A client's stated problem might be significantly exaggerated and
urgency stressed when it was relayed to the social worker on duty.
Again the client's interests were being looked after to ensure
contact.

The extent to which a receptionist was prepared to perform this function was dependent on a variety of factors. It was largely related to her own assessment of the needs of a particular client, or upon the opinion that the client was being treated inappropriately or unfairly by a child care officer. It may have depended simply on more personal considerations such as her likes and dislikes of certain individuals.

Whilst the advocacy function could be an important asset for visiting clients, the reverse process could also be seen. Clients could be suppressed in a variety of ways. As has been described, the receptionist conducted an initial interview identifying the reason for the visit. The subsequent telephone call to the social worker concerned might be used to exaggerate the urgency of the problem in an attempt to ensure that the client was seen. By the same token, the conversation between receptionist and social worker might understate the problem and result in delay before the client was seen. In the largest office, the simple withdrawal by the receptionist of her advocacy activities was sufficient, in many cases, for a client to be suppressed. The social work staff had become used to being continually reminded of the presence of visitors. When the reminders were not forthcoming, clients in the waiting-room were quickly forgotten. The suppression of clients was undertaken—frequently, I am sure, unconsciously—for equally undefined or trivial reasons to those which led to the promotion of some of their more fortunate counterparts.

The advocacy/suppression activities of receptionists had the effect of promoting or inhibiting the chances of a visiting client making contact with a social worker in the agency. At best a client suppressed by a receptionist would only result in a temporary delay in being seen; at worst a client might be prevented from seeing a social worker at all on that visit.

This form of restriction on client access should not be confused with the secretarial activities of receptionists where a client is delayed or 'put off' from seeing a social worker on a social worker's instructions. Here we are concerned with limitations on access introduced solely by the receptionists themselves for reasons of their own.

A third important reception service was the provision of advice and guidance. Reception staff were constantly faced with the problem of dealing with clients when no social worker was available. One reaction when faced with this difficulty was for receptionists to provide advice for the client in the absence of the help of a social worker. This may simply have involved the receptionist attempting to ensure that the officer saw the client at the earliest possible opportunity. It may have involved advising the client of other agencies which might be able to help, or even providing advice and guidance on the problem facing the client. This advisory role was a further logical extension of the initial interviewing function. Where a client had explained her problem to the receptionist and a social worker was unable to see her, the natural reaction of the receptionist was to advise as best she could in the absence of more professional assistance.

Receptionists and social workers

The role of the receptionists brought them constantly into contact with social work staff. They were used in different ways by social workers in each of the four offices. In small settings, in particular, where they were also responsible for the switchboard and telephone inquiries, part at least of their work was as clerical aide. Tasks such as making telephone calls for child care officers, fixing appointments, taking and giving messages and regulating the level of client flow were all commonplace and are usually associated with the reception process. The delegation of these tasks did, however, have the unanticipated consequence of enhancing the status of reception workers and encouraging their client-orientated activities as initial interviewers, advocates and quasi-professionals. Some of the dysfunctional consequences for clients of these activities have been described.

Whilst in all offices for most of the time there was a good relationship between social work and reception staff, in certain areas of their work they were constantly in suppressed, if not open, conflict. A better example of structural goal conflict would be difficult to find.

The reception staff saw their primary task as that of ensuring contact between a visiting client and a social worker. This might be possible with a single telephone call to the social worker; it might involve persistent calls before the client was eventually seen. It might necessitate the fixing of a specific appointment for some time in the future, telling a visitor on which day a particular social worker would definitely be in the office, or being able to say that the social worker would call at the client's home on a specified date.

For the social worker, particularly in the larger offices faced with a heavy client bombardment rate, interviewing visitors at the office was only a small part of their day-to-day activities. In a situation where a child care officer was already deeply involved with other things, interviewing a client in reception was considered more of an inconvenience than an important part of the work. Under these circumstances a visiting client might receive rather less attention that the reception staff thought they deserved.

The child care staff, faced with other problems on a duty day, tended to place the greater part of the responsibility for clients visiting the department upon the reception staff. This was perceived by the latter group as an attempt by the social worker to avoid his responsibility for the visiting client. Both parties were attempting to pursue their own primary objectives as they saw them. Neither party was fully aware of the pressures faced by the other, and were therefore unable to modify their own actions accordingly.

Some social workers delegated tasks to the reception staff which they themselves were unwilling or unable to perform. However, this practice was also functional for the receptionists, despite their criticism of the practice. This informal delegation of additional powers helped to increase their own job satisfaction whilst at the same time making it easier for them to deal with difficult situations when they arose. In the process receptionists were drawn even further into the social work activities of the agency.

THE RECEPTION FUNCTION

Whilst the details of reception activities in the case-studies vary there are large areas of similarity. Receptionists performed a series of important functions for both the professional staff and the clients of the organisation. *For clients* they were the first point of contact with the agency and in most cases undertook an initial interview; they advised and redirected clients who were themselves often not sure of their needs; they acted as advocates for those whom they considered were being treated inappropriately or unfairly by the field staff and warranted special attention. At the same time the receptionists provided basic services *for child care officers*. They suppressed and otherwise dealt with difficult clients; they regulated the flow of bombardment and provided a means by which social workers could avoid direct conflict with their clientele.

In short, reception staff acted as a powerful 'buffer' between field workers and their clients and potential clients and as such exerted a considerable influence on the provision of primary agency services. Far from performing only a passive function within the organisation, receptionists were frequently operating very much in the area of professional judgement and discretion.

RECEPTIONIST-CLIENT INVOLVEMENT

Throughout the analysis of reception activities repeated reference has been made to the concept of *receptionist-client involvement*. This has been used very simply as a blanket term to cover all those elements of the reception function which involve interaction between receptionist and visitor over and above the minimum necessary to establish contact between a service provider and a potential recipient. Thus it includes all initial reception interviewing activities, advocacy and suppression, and the range of additional reception services identified.

A very high degree of involvement with clients was the most striking feature of the receptionist's role in two of the offices studied, and occurred in a more limited form in a third. The absence of overt forms of involvement in the fourth office, Cassford, serves to underline the impact of its presence in the other three, and provides important clues as to why involvement occurs.

Any attempt to isolate the main causal variables is fraught with difficulties. The sheer complexity of the elements involved in the different settings makes it very difficult to summarise and evaluate their impact outside the context of the particular agencies in which they were observed. Any generalisation about causation inevitably fails to take adequate account of the peculiar circumstances in any one office, or of the influence of a series of factors acting in combination, and interacting with each other. With these reservations in mind, however, I have attempted to isolate and summarise some of the key variables which appear from the case studies to be causally related to receptionist-client involvement. It seems likely that in a reception setting in which a high proportion of these variables are present, the level of receptionist involvement with clients will be correspondingly high. In cases (such as Cassford) in which certain key elements are absent, involvement is likely to be at a minimum.

SUMMARY OF FACTORS PRODUCING INVOLVEMENT

1. FORMAL INTAKE PROCEDURES
   Ensuring the 'appropriateness' of a visit
   Completing an Initial Inquiry Form
   Assessing the degree of urgency of an inquiry

2. QUASI-FORMAL INSTRUCTIONS
   Negative feedback
   Requests for additional information
   Requests to deal with visitors in a particular way
   Message taking and giving

3. THE NATURE OF THE RECEPTION OFFICE
   Service and non-service reception
   Ambiguity/complexity of reception

4. THE DEGREE OF DIFFICULTY IN ESTABLISHING SOCIAL
   WORKER-CLIENT CONTACTS
   Factors influencing social worker accessibility

1. *Formal intake procedures*
For the most part activities of reception staff were not officially prescribed. Of the few tasks which they were specifically asked to perform, several had the unanticipated consequence of receptionist involvement with visitors. Three tasks in particular were common to Borough, New Town and West County and were directly related to the extent to which receptionists questioned visitors about their reasons for coming to the office.

Ensuring the 'appropriateness' of a visit   Reception staff are usually expected to ensure that visitors to their office have come to the right place to deal with their particular inquiry or problem. In the complex field of social welfare this may involve a fairly detailed discussion of a visitor's reason for calling before the appropriateness of an inquiry can be ascertained. In an office where this task is stressed and reinforced by social work staff when an 'error' is made, receptionists are under considerable pressure to ensure that an 'inappropriate' request for help does not get past the reception desk.

Completing an Initial Inquiry Form   The prescribed task of completing a more or less detailed inquiry form for every new applicant
I

inevitably necessitates the receptionist conducting an initial contact interview. In the first instance the depth of the interview is likely to be directly related to the amount of detail required to complete the form. Once such an interviewing practice is established, however, it may be further extended to include known as well as new clients.

Assessing the degree of urgency of an inquiry Reception staff are frequently asked to disturb a duty officer, or to interrupt a meeting only if an inquiry is urgent. Urgency can frequently be assessed to the receptionist's satisfaction only after discussing the problem being presented. Again, an initial reception interview is made necessary by asking the receptionist to make this kind of decision. In some offices 'unnecessary' interruptions of meetings are severely frowned upon and the receptionist's tendency to interview and discuss problems is further reinforced.

2. *Quasi-formal instructions*
Instructions and comments to reception staff from social workers and others represent a further series of pressures towards involvement.

Negative feedback Reference has already been made in the summary of reception activities to the reinforcing effect of negative feedback or implied criticism of inappropriate or non-urgent cases being referred through to a social worker 'unnecessarily'. This has the effect of increasing a receptionist's determination to filter more effectively in future, and therefore to get more involved with clients in order to do so.

In addition, social workers place a series of more direct pressures on receptionists to get involved by instructions and requests of various kinds.

Requests for additional information In most offices receptionists contact members of the social work staff by internal telephone to inform them that a visitor is in Reception to see them. In a very high proportion of the many calls of this kind observed during the study, the social worker asked the receptionist for further information about the visitor before agreeing to an interview. To provide this additional information, the receptionist necessarily had to question the visitor further—sometimes about very personal details, the disclosure of which to a receptionist caused obvious distress on the part of the client. This information was then relayed back to the social worker, who then might or might not interview the visitor personally.

The extent of this practice appears to vary directly in relation to the physical distance between the reception desk and the social worker's office. In New Town where most social work staff were literally only a few paces from Reception, supplementary questions were largely unnecessary, although they were occasionally still asked, because it was almost as easy to step out of their room and see a client personally. In Borough, on the other hand, half of the social work staff were situated four floors away from the reception area, and constant trips up and down in the lift were seen as something of an inconvenience. Here the social workers constantly asked reception staff to get additional information in order to establish whether or not an interview with a social worker was really necessary. At times it appeared that the social worker was attempting to conduct an interview with a waiting client over the internal telephone, using the receptionist as an intermediary to repeat the social worker's questions and relay back the answers.

It is significant that in Borough there was a striking difference in the extent of this practice between social workers situated on the fifth floor of the office block, and those who worked on the same floor as Reception. In the latter case, the number of supplementary questions which receptionists were expected to put at the point of initial inquiry were very much fewer than their colleagues on the fifth floor expected.

Requests to deal with visitors in a particular way Receptionists in all offices received instructions from the social work staff as to how they should perform their task in relation to particular individuals or groups, or at particular times. These might be 'standing instructions' (e.g. not to disturb any meeting unless there is a 'crisis' or an urgent inquiry) which are generally recognised by all the social workers; they might by 'temporary instructions' given by one social worker to operate for only a limited period (e.g. 'No one at all to disturb me for the next two hours', or 'If Mrs —— calls again find out what she wants and tell her I'll call'). These kinds of prescribed task frequently place the reception worker in a position where she feels unable to do anything but respond to visitor's requests for help and/or give advice herself in the absence of a social worker.

In a few cases observed, social workers instructed a receptionist to respond directly to a particular visitor's inquiry. One case, referred to in Chapter 3, involved a child care officer asking the receptionist to tell a particular visitor if she called that he was not going to receive her child into care, and the reasons why. As the receptionist observed, 'It's a bit much'.

Message taking and giving A common practice in several of the offices was to ask reception staff to give messages to, and accept messages from, visitors who called in the absence of their social worker. Where such messages involved the substantive content of a client's problem (or other reason for contacting the agency) the receptionist was frequently involved in discussion about this contact with the visitor—either in explaining a message from the social worker, or in ensuring that she had collected sufficient information from the client to give the social worker a useful message on his or her return.

The crucial element here is the amount of detail which the social work staff indicate they expect messages to contain. In New Town, for example, where only a limited explanation of the reason of a client's visit was expected the taking of the message was itself one reason for the low level of involvement. Accepting messages was one way in which the receptionist could demonstrate that she was doing something for the client, and this represented an important alternative to involvement.

In Cassford and Borough, on the other hand, social worker expectations about the degree of detail in messages were far higher and the writing of messages for social workers necessitated a higher degree of involvement than would otherwise have been necessary.

3. *Nature of the reception office*
A large number of factors relating to the type, structure, layout, size and location of the reception office itself appear to have a considerable impact upon the extent and of receptionist-client involvement. The primary effect of many of these features is to increase the difficulty of establishing contact between social worker and client. For this reason most structural elements have been classified under Section 4 below. However, two aspects of the reception office's structure and type appear to have a *direct* impact on involvement.

Service and non-service reception The distinction between a *service-orientated* and a *non-service* receptionist was made as a result of the analysis of reception in the West County town hall. Here the general, non-service receptionist had the responsibility for directing visitors to departments and rooms which they required, and not (as with service-orientated receptionists) for establishing contact between a visitor and a particular individual. The non-service receptionist was thus not subjected to the many pressures towards involvement which faced service receptionists as a result of the difficulties they experienced in establishing contact between clients' particular social workers (discussed below). In addition she was not exposed to the negative feedback about clients she misdirected as there was little direct contact with the personnel of any of the departments she served. She was able as a result to refer visitors to departments or rooms on the basis of certain key words used by the visitor in making their initial statement about their reasons for visiting. Supplementary questions were rarely necessary.

Other things being equal, therefore, I would hypothesise that the non-service receptionist, however wide-ranging the inquiries with which she is faced is less likely to become involved with visitors than is the service-orientated receptionists. The degree of her involvement with visitors would be likely to increase in direct proportion to the amount of negative feedback she received from agency staff and visitors alike about directing visitors to the 'wrong' department or room.

Ambiguity/Complexity of Reception I have just argued that however wide ranging the types of inquiry faced by a non-service receptionist in the absence of negative feedback a high degree of involvement with visitors is unlikely. The range of inquiries faced by a *service-orientated receptionist*, however, is an extremely important determinant of involvement. In the Borough case-study, for example, reception staff were faced with clients of both the health and the children's departments and, in theory at least, were responsible for putting visitors in touch with particular staff members of each of these departments. A fairly detailed interview was often necessary in order to establish both which department was required and which individual was the best person to contact. The contact then had to be established. In this kind of work initial 'accuracy' was seen to be very important as the reception staff themselves faced the repercussions of a wrong referral.

The greater the number of different departments or sections served by a service-orientated receptionist (i.e. responsible for establishing person-to-person contacts), the greater the level of involvement is likely to be.

The tendency is increased in a reception office which is ambiguously placed or signposted. The greater the ambiguity, the greater the number of callers at the office who have come to the wrong place is likely to be. As a result, reception staff quickly become aware of the need to interview all-comers, at least briefly, in order to establish the appropriateness of the visit. In a single-purpose office, such as New Town, which is very well and obviously signposted, the number of incorrect inquiries is very few and an initial sifting interview is rarely seen to be necessary. The few incorrect inquiries are usually identified quickly on the basis of the visitors opening remarks.

4. *The degree of difficulty in establishing social worker-client contacts*
The degree of difficulty faced by receptionists in establishing contact between a visitor and a social worker is probably the most important of all the factors identified. The primary task of the receptionist is to establish a contact, either at the time or in the future, between the service provider and the potential recipient of a service. Difficulties in establishing such a meeting lead to pressures on the receptionist as intermediary to 'fill the gap' and provide substitute advice or assistance, or to act as an advocate by pressuring for some alternative form of service (e.g. an interview with an absent social worker's colleague).

In an office such as New Town where, for a variety of reasons, little difficulty was experienced by reception staff in establishing social worker-client contacts, the level of involvement remained low. In Borough and West County where establishing contact was a major problem, involvement was developed to a very high degree. It was largely avoided in Cassford by ensuring that there was always someone on hand other than the receptionist to deal with inquiries. Evidence from the case-studies, therefore, suggests that, other things being equal, the greater the degree of difficulty faced by receptionists in establishing social worker-client contacts, the higher will be the level of receptionist-client involvement.

Factors influencing social worker accessibility Throughout the case-studies a large number of factors have been identified as directly or indirectly increasing the difficulty of establishing social worker-client contacts. Some of these were considered in detail in the 'Discussion' section of Chapter 4. They include amongst others: size and layout of the building; size of social work staff; level of client bombardment on the reception office; extent to which informal rationing mechanisms are used by social work staff; degree of priority vested in 'duty' work; extent to which an effective appointment system is used; extent to which social workers accurately recorded their whereabouts in the office 'diary'; office practices in restricting access (during supervision sessions, meetings, lunch and coffee times etc.); temporary or permanent inability of the agency to cope with bombardment levels (e.g. during holidays); structure of the agency's intake system; social workers' attitudes to the reception and intake process. Any one or more of these factors acting in combination may operate in any situation to make it difficult for receptionists to establish contacts between visitors and a member of the agency's staff.

One general point is clearly illustrated by this analysis. The nature of an agency's entire reception, intake and allocation system, and not just the type of reception arrangements, is a crucial determinant of the extent to which a receptionist is likely to be pressured into involvement. The way in which an intake system is defined in total may to a large extent predetermine the role to be played by the reception worker.

RESPONSES TO RECEPTIONIST-CLIENT INVOLVEMENT

This book has described and analysed some of the effects of the activities of reception staff in a social work agency on the provision of services to clients. It has shown the impact reception workers may have on decisions about who receives what services, when, from whom and for how long. For practitioners in the social services who do not see receptionist-client involvement of the kind described as being in any way problematic, the foregoing analysis may have served to help them more clearly to recognise the true nature of the receptionists' role, and some of the problems they face in performing their tasks. To practitioners who view the phenomenon of involvement as a problem, the case-studies provide indications of a number of practical steps which might be taken to reduce the impact of the gatekeeper on decision-making. Two extreme responses may be seen to occupy the opposite ends of a continuum.

Trained social worker as receptionist

At one extreme the reception function might be performed by a trained social worker. Quite simply, the traditional untrained clerical receptionist might be replaced by a member of the social work staff who would then perform very much the same kind of role as that described for any of the receptionists in the case-studies. With no corresponding alterations in the structural context of client reception, such a worker would be faced with very similar pressures to those of her clerical predecessor, but would, it is hoped, be better equipped to respond to these pressures in an appropriate way. In some social service department area offices, the receptionist has already been replaced by one or two 'duty' social workers and early reports suggest that this can work very well. This is especially so, if the reception desk is linked closely with a team of full-time intake (or short-term) workers. Such a solution to the reception intake problem is rapidly gaining credibility in social service departments; a number have already established intake groups as a priority in departmental policy.

The counter-arguments to a social worker as receptionist are obvious. Most frequent of these, and possibly the most powerful, is that given shortages of trained staff, those who exist could be better deployed on work other than client reception. The weight given to this and other arguments depends on the degree of priority one is willing to give to ensuring that clients and potential clients receive appropriate help and are not rationed out or inequitably promoted at the point of initial contact. One way of ensuring that the reception and intake process is given the importance it deserves would be to invest far more resources in it than at present.

Clerical receptionist with a limited role

At the other end of the continuum, the reception function might continue to be performed by a clerical worker but in the context of an intake system which limits the extent of available discretion, and minimises the structural pressures towards involvement. Inadvertently, this was what had been done in Cassford. Here, many of the pressures which produced involvement in Borough, West County and New Town were not present by virtue of the way in which the reception process had been defined within the total intake system. Once the key factors which produce receptionist involvement in an agency have been identified, the reception and intake process can be modified in order to remove the pressures. Thus even in an agency which has no option but to retain non-professional reception personnel, a great deal can be done to limit the extent of their gatekeeping power. In some cases much improvement could be achieved simply by rebriefing certain members of the staff and increasing their awareness of some of the dysfunctional consequences of their actions; in others major structural and procedural changes might be necessary.

A few examples will help to clarify the kinds of action which might be taken. The Initial Inquiry Form which many receptionists are required to complete may invoke a reception interview. Such a form is usually needed for three reasons: to find out who the person is; to identify whether or not they have contacted the department before; and to establish geographical eligibility for a service. Frequently, in addition, a form completed at this stage in the intake process acts as a front sheet in any subsequent file. All the information a receptionist needs for these purposes at the initial inquiry stage is the client's name, address and whether or not they have had contact with the agency before. This is sufficient information to trace the necessary files, and to establish geographical eligibility. If, therefore, having collected this small amount of information, the client is asked to wait, searches can be undertaken by a duty or intake social worker. At this stage in the intake process the relevance of an application can be established and further information about the client and his or her reason for calling can be collected by the social worker during the first interview. In the Cassford office, the restriction of the receptionist's role in this way was an important factor in limiting the level of involvement and did not appear to reduce her ability to filter out the callers who had obviously come to the wrong building. These were easily identified by the opening statements or requests.

Known clients can be dealt with in exactly the same way. With this minimum information the receptionist is able, while the client is in the waiting room, to trace the relevant social worker. When the social worker is not available, without further contact with the client the receptionist calls upon a duty or intake worker, who then sees the client. This social worker is then in a position to take any appropriate action. Such a change in procedure would have the added advantage of removing from the receptionist the responsibility for assessing the urgency of an inquiry. If more automatic referrals of visitors to a duty or intake officer were made in this way, a further important pressure towards involvement would be removed.

This leads to a more general point. I have strongly argued throughout that a major determinant of the level of receptionist-client involvement was the degree of difficulty experienced by the receptionist in establishing contact with a social worker or other service provider. Where contact was difficult to achieve, the receptionist frequently felt it necessary to respond in a positive way to a client's needs. One important way of counteracting this tendency is to ensure that an intake system is defined in such depth that there are always recognised alternatives to involvement for the receptionist to use. For example, when a client calls at an office and the relevant social worker is not available, it could be an established procedure that such a client is automatically referred through to a duty officer, and not on the basis of the receptionist's assessment of urgency. If all the duty officers are otherwise engaged, a duty senior could be available, again automatically, to see the visitor. And so on. If sufficient care is taken when defining reception procedures to provide a series of recognised alternatives which the receptionist should take with each inquiry as a matter of course, many of the more striking manifestations of involvement would no longer be necessary.

To minimise the dysfunctional consequences of comments, instructions and criticisms of reception staff by social workers, one might rely on the simple explanation of the effects of such reactions on reception practice. A social work team aware of the difficulties faced by reception staff is far less likely to increase this burden by informal rationing practices. Some discussion and agreement between social work and reception staff, using the expertise, knowledge and experience of both groups, might produce valuable changes in the intake practices of both receptionists and social workers alike.

In addition, a number of straightforward changes could easily be introduced into the reception process. Improvements in procedures for recording the present and future whereabouts of social workers would help a great deal, particularly if every worker had an established day, say, once a week, when the receptionist knew they would be in the office and available for visitors. Similarly, social work staff could ensure that one of their number is always available to see visitors at any time, whether or not a caller has had the misfortune to call during a meeting, a lunch- or coffee-break.

It is very evident therefore, that if the level of receptionist-client involvement is thought to be problematic there are a number of practical steps that can be taken—some quite quickly and easily—to reduce the worst excesses of the reception desk. As ever in a problem situation such as this a quick incremental response may be very effective and produce beneficial results. But such a response may result in client reception continuing to be seen in isolation from the rest of the agency's operations. In the long term if the problems inherent in the client reception process are to be tackled, reception must be seen within the context of the whole process of client intake, assessment and allocation.

This analysis of reception practices clearly demonstrates that pressures on reception staff to become increasingly involved with clients derive largely from shortcomings and breakdowns in the client intake system of which the initial reception process is just a small part. These in turn are frequently the result of a basic and fundamental problem in any social work agency: the absence of a systematic approach to defining priorities which provides a rational basis for allocation of resources—accepting, rejecting and closing cases. Without such a system, as I argued in the Introduction, decisions about resource allocation and service provision tend to be made not on the basis of rational choice, but as a result of non-rational factors such as client pressures and chance. One of the many elements which may affect decisions about who receives what services is the person who looks after the telephone or sits behind the reception desk.

Appendix A

CLIENT BOMBARDMENT FORM

RECEPTION   DATE. . . . .
TIME OF ARRIVAL. . . . .
TIME SEEN (OR DEPARTED UNSEEN). . . . .

NAME: . . . .   CHILDREN'S
ADDRESS: . . . .   HEALTH
          . . . .   OTHER: Specify
          . . . .

If the client is applying to the children's department:

1. Has this client contacted this department before?   YES | NO

2. If YES: How many times?   1 or 2 | SEVERAL | MANY

How recently?   . . . .

Child care officer informed		Seen by own child care officer	
Unable to help		Seen by duty officer	
Referred to receptionist to (specify):		Not seen: message left	
		Not seen: no message	

Appendix B

COMPARATIVE TABLE OF KEY VARIABLES

	Client Bombardment[a] Children's Dept Visitors per Week	All Visitors per Week	Number of Reception Staff	Number of Social Workers	Duties of Receptionist	Type of Building	Population Covered by Office	Degree of Receptionist-Client Involvement
BOROUGH	270	414	2/3	50	receptionist for health and children's departments, post	3rd floor in a 10-storey office block	320,000	high
NEW TOWN	41	41	1[b]	12	receptionist and telephonist for area office, typing and misc. duties	converted 18th-century dwelling house	64,000	low
WEST COUNTY[c]	53	53	1	13	chief clerk, receptionist for area office	suite of rooms in town hall	112,000	medium/high
CASSFORD	45	51	1	30	receptionist and telephonist for area office, typing and misc. duties	purpose-built in 1961-2 with later extensions	185,000	very low

a Numbers of client units visiting each office. Weekly average of two weeks.
b Two receptionists employed—one in the mornings, one in the afternoons.
c Information refers to receptionist in the area office, not in the entrance to the town hall.

SELECTED BIBLIOGRAPHY

CLIENT RECEPTION

BESSELL, R., *Interviewing and Counselling* (Batsford, 1971).

BLAU, P. M., 'Orientations towards Clients in a Public Welfare Agency', *Administrative Science Quarterly* (1960), Vol. 5, pp. 341–61. Also in Zald, M. N. (ed.), *Social Welfare Institutions* (Wiley, New York, 1965).
The Dynamics of Bureaucracy: A Study of Interpersonal Relations in Two Government Agencies (Chicago University Press, revised edn, 1963).

BLAU, P. M. AND SCOTT, W. R., *Formal Organisations* (Routledge & Kegan Paul, 1963).

CAMMOCK, R. M., *Health Centres Reception, Waiting and Patient Call* (HMSO, 1973).

DEUTSCHER, I., 'The Gatekeeper in Public Housing', in Deutscher, I. and Thompson, E. J. (eds), *Among the People: Encounters with the Poor* (Basic Books, New York, 1968).

FORSYTH, G., LOGAN, R. et al., *Gateway or Dividing Line? A study of Hospital Out-patients in the 1960s* (Nuffield Provincial Hospitals Trust Series', Oxford University Press, 1968).

HALL, A. S., 'Client Reception in a Social Service Agency', *Public Administration* (Spring 1971).
'The Role of the Receptionist', *Municipal Journal* (10 March 1972).

HILL, M. J., 'The Exercise of Discretion in the National Assistance Board', *Public Administration* (Spring 1969).

KEMENY, P. J. AND POPPLESTONE, G., 'Client Discrimination in Social Welfare Agencies', *Social Work* (April 1970), Vol. 27, No. 2, pp. 7–15.

LEISSNER, A., *Family Advice Services* (National Children's Bureau; Longman, 1967).

Report of the Committee on Local Authority and Allied Personal Social Services (Seebohm Committee) (HMSO, 1968), Cmnd 3703.

INTAKE

APLIN, D. O., 'The Intake Group: a Continuing Experiment in the Team Approach', *Case Conference* (October 1968).

BORGATTA, E. F., FANSHEL, D. AND MEYER, H. J., *Social Workers' Perceptions of Clients* (Russell Sage Foundation, New York, 1960).

DAY, P. R., 'Perception and Social Work Tasks', *Probation* (November 1972), Vol. 18, No. 3.

DE SCHWEINITZ, K. AND E., *Interviewing in the Social Services* (National Council of Social Service, 1962).

DUNCAN, T. M., 'Intake in an Integrated Team', *Health and Social Services Journal* (10 February 1973).

FRANCIS, R. G. AND STONE, R. C., *Service and Procedure within a Bureaucracy* (Minneapolis, Minnesota University Press, 1956).

GEORGE, V. AND HAZEL, N., 'The Work of Two Children's Departments', *Social Work* (January 1970), Vol. 27, No. 1, pp. 23–5.

HALL, A. S., 'An Analysis of the Work of a Local Authority Children's Department *vis-à-vis* its New Clients' (1970: Mimeo. NISW Library).

HEYMAN, M., 'Criteria for the Allocation of Cases According to the levels of Staff Skills', *Social Casework* (USA, July 1961), Vol. 42, No. 7.

MAYER, J. AND TIMMS, N., 'Clash in Perspective between Worker and Client', *Social Casework* (USA, January 1969), Vol. 50, No. 1, pp. 32–40.

MULLEN, E. J., 'Casework Communication', *Social Casework* (USA, November 1968), Vol. 49, No. 9, pp. 546–51.
'The Relationship between Diagnosis and Treatment in Casework', *Social Casework* (USA, April 1969), Vol. 50, No. 4, pp. 218–26.
'Differences in Worker Style in Casework', *Social Casework* (USA, June 1969), Vol. 50, No. 6, pp. 347–53.

PARKER, R. A., 'Social Administration and Scarcity—The Problem of Rationing', *Social Work* (April 1967), Vol. 24, No. 2, pp. 9–14.

PARNICKY, J. J. *et al.*, 'A Study of the Effectiveness of Referrals', *Social Casework* (USA, December 1961), Vol. 42, No. 10, pp. 490–501.

PERLMAN, H. H., 'Intake and Some Role Considerations', *Social Casework* (USA, April 1960), Vol. 41, No. 4, pp. 171–9.

REES, A. M., 'Access to the Personal Health and Welfare Services', *Social and Economic Administration* (January 1972), Vol. 6, No. 1, pp. 34–43.

REID, W. AND SHYNE, A., *Brief and Extended Casework* (Columbia University Press, 1969).

REID, W. AND EPSTEIN, L., *Task-Centred Casework* (Columbia University Press, 1972).

ROSENBLATT, A., 'The Application of Role Concepts to the Intake Process', *Social Casework* (USA, January 1962), Vol. 43, No. 1, pp. 8–14.

SERVICE, P. D., 'The Use of Intake Systems in Hospitals', *Medical Social Work* (1968–9), Vol. 21, pp. 308–13.

SHYNE, A. W., 'What Research Tells Us about Short-Term Cases in Family Agencies', *Social Casework* (USA, May 1957), Vol. 38, No. 5, pp. 223–31.

SILVERMAN, P. R., 'A Re-examination of Intake Procedure', *Social Casework* (USA, December 1970), Vol. 51, No. 10, pp. 625–34.
STARK, F. B., 'Barriers to Client-Worker Communication at Intake', *Social Casework* (USA, April 1959), Vol. 40, No. 5, pp. 177–83.
STEVENS, A. G., 'Rationing in the Social Services', *The Welfare Officer* (1972).

INDEX

Printed and bound by CPI Group (UK) Ltd, Croydon, CR0 4YY

17/10/2024

01775689-0012